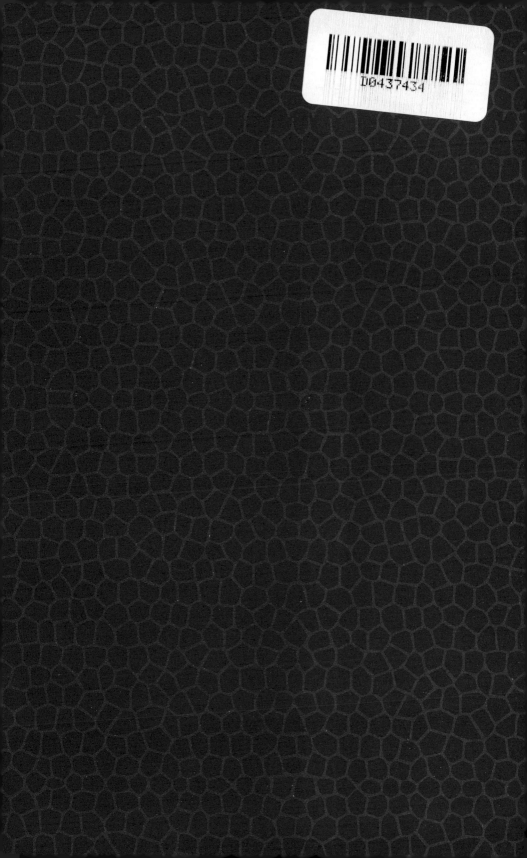

of
MEDICINE,
MIRACLES,
and
MINDSETS

MOSAICA PRESS

of

MEDICINE, MIRACLES, *and* MINDSETS

One family's fight for their baby's life...
and the lessons learned along the way

Elie and Chaya Rochel Estrin

Published by Mosaica Press, Inc.
www.mosaicapress.com
info@mosaicapress.com

Advance Praise

A LOPSIDED BATTLE for a baby's life, a struggle to cope with the medically uncharted, and an account of faith and wonder fed by modern miracles. Honesty and emotion, humor and pragmatism, a meticulous journal of medical conditions and procedures set to persistently dueling tunes of family life and medical emergencies.

This is a masterful work of spiritual and professional value: it is a stinging rebuke of unforgivable attitudes plaguing medical practice; a demonstration of the role faith and positivism play amid practical realities; a stirring salute to the Healer of all flesh, Whose interventions are too loud to deny; and a meaningful guide to doctors and patients alike, based on the value of life and dignity and on the pioneering approach to medicine illuminated by the Lubavitcher Rebbe.

Rabbi Efraim Mintz, director, Rohr Jewish Learning Institute

IN ADDITION to being a profoundly personal and breathtakingly honest account of a family that was open to—and received—countless miracles, this book provides long-needed and absolutely invaluable advice for medical providers, families, and friends who encounter such heartrending, and heartsoaring, circumstances. Simultaneously deeply spiritual and deeply practical, I recommend this book to anyone facing the sorts of challenges we would never wish on another.

Dr. Sarah Stroup, Professor of Classics, University of Washington;
fellow parent to a cardiac survivor

A GREAT STORY, but perhaps more importantly a valuable primer for medical professionals. Heartily recommended for medical students and doctors of all levels and specialties.

Stanley M. Fried, MD, Family Medicine, Long Beach, CA

THIS POIGNANT STORY is much more than a medical roller coaster. It is a case study in how the patient-physician-family relationship can go wrong and how the determination of a family can make all of the difference in complex health encounters. A worthwhile read for both medical professionals and families going through tough health situations.

Jeffrey Levsky, MD, PhD, Professor of Cardiothoracic Radiology and Medicine/ Cardiology, Montefiore Medical Center / Albert Einstein College of Medicine

RABBI ESTRIN has written an important book that will be very helpful to parents going through difficult medical episodes with one of their children. An easy read, the combination of humor and practical advice will assist many in dealing with their own life situation.

Rabbi Aaron E. Glatt, MD, associate rabbi, Young Israel of Woodmere; Chair of Medicine, Mount Sinai South Nassau; professor, Icahn School of Medicine at Mount Sinai

INCREDIBLE...The narrative is compelling, the world-view invaluable, and the writing top-notch. *Of Medicine, Miracles, and Mindsets* deserves to be read by a wide audience.

Rabbi Avi Shafran, Director of Public Affairs and spokesman, Agudath Israel of America

RIVETING, very honest and straightforward...Very moving to see how you stood up against all odds and against medical cold analysis so many times in order to give Nissi the best fighting chance.

Rabbi Sholly Weiser, Yaldei Shluchei HaRebbe

AN extraordinary journey.

Ellen Weiss, MSW, former Chai LifeLine SE director

I WANT to acknowledge the resolute determination and resiliency that the Estrins had in order to take the necessary route at many critical junctures in Nissi's medical journey—always with steadfast faith, trust, and most impressively, joy. Different parents react to crisis in different ways, and the approach taken by the Estrins was impressive and inspirational.

Rabbi Yosef Marlow, rabbi, Beis Menachem of North Miami Beach

MOVING and ultimately inspiring. Through the power of this story, you feel personally connected to wonderful and Godly people.

Michael Medved, radio host, author of God's Hand on America

VERY COMPELLING and bravely written. I could not put it down.

Rabbi Yosef Friedman, director, Kehot Publication Society

A GRIPPING TALE of perseverance and not taking no for an answer...A manual for proactive faith in G-d, [and] a must-read for every parent.

Rabbi Yisroel Edelman, rabbi, Young Israel of Deerfield Beach

I AM OVERWHELMED by the grace and beauty of your parenting under such challenging circumstances.

Nancy Zaretsky, MA, inclusion specialist, Greater Miami Jewish Federation

RABBI ELIE ESTRIN and his wife Chaya have written a soul-searching book that takes us through a very human journey. If you want to experience life-all-in-one book, this is the one.

Howard Behar, president Starbucks, retired

NISSI'S STORY leaves the reader in awe of the formidable power that faith and love wield in his parents' fight for their child's life against all medical expectations.

Baila Olidort, editor-in-chief, Lubavitch International Magazine

HEARTFELT, heart-rending, and heart-warming all at once. I know it was meaningful for me, and I know I'm not alone. Well-done and thanks again!

Lt Gen Mike Plehn, USAF

VERY MOVING and well-written...I personally benefited from reading Rabbi Estrin's book. As a doctor, I found it exciting and medically well-documented, and as a Jew, I found its life lessons valuable. The book has very good advice for people going through similar crises—shared from deep personal experience.

Rabbi Dr. Akiva Tatz, founder, the Jerusalem Medical Ethics Forum

A BREATHTAKING and miraculous story, a steady flow of incredible providence at every juncture. This book contains ample lessons for the medical provider, and is a must-read for those treating patients with long odds.

Yitzy Shollar, PA-C

WHEN given an unexpected diagnosis for a child, whether at birth or a mental health condition later on in life, parents and family members' lives take a drastic turn...How a family copes, advocates, and eventually thrives with children with differing needs is often a result of a combination of community and familial support, personal and learned perspective, an openness and willingness for help and direction, perseverance, and above all, acceptance with love. This book helps to start the process from the very beginning by placing family members in a position of knowledge, strength, and support.

Dr. Sarah Kranz-Ciment, PT, DPT

In honor of

Rabbi Yitzchak Meir
and Leah Lipszyc

THEIR CHILDREN

In memory of

Chaplain Gary Friedman

חיים צבי בן יהודה לייב ז״ל

Yahrtzeit, 30 Shevat 5776

הוּא הָיָה אוֹמֵר, עֲשֵׂה רְצוֹנוֹ כִרְצוֹנֶךָ, כְּדֵי שֶׁיַּעֲשֶׂה רְצוֹנְךָ כִרְצוֹנוֹ.

בַּטֵּל רְצוֹנְךָ מִפְּנֵי רְצוֹנוֹ, כְּדֵי שֶׁיְּבַטֵּל רְצוֹן אֲחֵרִים מִפְּנֵי רְצוֹנֶךָ.

הִלֵּל אוֹמֵר, אַל תִּפְרשׁ מִן הַצִּבּוּר, וְאַל תַּאֲמִין בְּעַצְמְךָ עַד יוֹם מוֹתֶךָ,

וְאַל תָּדִין אֶת חֲבֵרְךָ עַד שֶׁתַּגִּיעַ לִמְקוֹמוֹ.

Pirkei Avot 2:4

THE CHABAD HOUSE MINYAN
www.ChabadHouseMinyan.org

Table of Contents

Part II

REFLECTIONS FOR MEDICAL PERSONNEL, FAMILIES, AND FRIENDS

Note for the Reader

The story you are about to read is true, although some names have been changed. While the narrative is told in Elie's voice—as it was originally written in a timeline overview of the events, intended for personal use—Chaya Rochel is an equal partner in the book's creation in every way. Her voice and feelings have been incorporated into the text throughout the book. We opted to keep Elie's first-person storytelling for simplification. All conversations herein are based on the best of our mutual understanding and recollection. Note, as well, that Chaya Rochel is referred to by just her first name throughout the book.

We have attempted to explain any foreign or medical terms when used the first time, but for a more detailed explanation, please refer to the glossary.

Prologue

A remarkable conversation between Rabbi Menachem M. Schneerson, the Lubavitcher Rebbe, and Dr. Mordechai Shani, director of Sheba Medical Center at Tel HaShomer Hospital, Israel's largest hospital, echoes in my mind. The two men met in the fall of 1976 and spoke extensively about the world of medicine. At the very outset of their first meeting, Rabbi Schneerson rejected usage of the modern Hebrew term for the word hospital, *beit cholim,* which would be translated literally as a "place for the ill."[1] Instead, he expressed his opinion that hospitals should become known as *batei refuah,* "places of healing."

HOSPITALS FIGURE PROMINENTLY in my childhood. I was born in Providence, Rhode Island, as the third of a family of seven children. My oldest brother, Rafi, had cystic fibrosis (CF). My parents protected us from the gory details of Rafi's disease, giving us as normal a childhood as can possibly be expected under the circumstances, but there was no avoiding the constant reality of the violent coughing and vomiting spells, or the frequent hospital stays.

We moved to Pittsburgh, Pennsylvania, when I was almost ten, and met a family living just down the street from us with a boy of their own with CF—Mikey Butler. Despite their four-year age difference and wide gap in life attitudes (Rafi the fighter, Mikey the politician), Rafi and Mikey would become close friends. My friends and I would often make

---

1   Interview with Jewish Educational Media, "Here's My Story," 14 Sept. 2016: http://my-encounterblog.com/?p=2391#more-2391.

the three-mile trek on Shabbat to visit one or both of them in the hospital, spending the duration of Shabbat in their hospital room or the floor teen lounge, talking, laughing, and more than anything else, debating.

In August 1997, Rafi was rushed to the hospital with an infection in his already terribly scarred lungs. Rafi's three weeks in the ICU—virtually comatose—were a different beast than what I had been used to. All we could see of his life were the indecipherable numbers on the screens above his bed, and his chest heaving under the pressure of the ventilator. The stress on our family was unbelievable as the doctors fought for his life. On the tenth of September, Rafi passed away. He was just twenty-two years old.

After that, understandably, I really didn't want to have anything to do with hospitals. Prior to his death, as a young teen, in those simple days before the institution of privacy laws limiting outsider access to patient information, I would spend the holidays of Rosh Hashanah and Sukkos running across town to Pittsburgh's hospitals, clambering from one floor to another to bring the sound of the shofar and the Four Species to the sick, but after Rafi's death I avoided those "routes." In 2003 I married Chaya Rochel, née Karp, and within our first year of marriage, we moved to Seattle to serve the Jews at the University of Washington as Chabad representatives. In the early stages of our work there, the idea of assisting Jews at the hospital as a chaplain came up, with its possibility of supplementing our small income, but I was not terribly interested in spending any more time in hospitals than I already had.

Things changed on January 27, 2005. I was blissfully playing Ping-Pong with a university student. The score was 6–2; Joey's six-foot wingspan had always had an edge over my smaller five-foot-six frame.

Suddenly my wife called me urgently from the other room. She was evidently going into preterm labor, at just twenty-six weeks, despite her pregnancy being just barely visible on her petite figure. We sped to the hospital—narrowly avoiding a head-on crash on the way—and six hours later, our eldest son was born. He was pint-sized, weighing just one pound, fifteen ounces (883 grams), and measuring fourteen inches (35.6 centimeters) long. Chaya, despite being the oldest of ten, had never experienced the hospital prior to this, and I calmed her as we went to the Neonatal Intensive Care Unit (NICU) to meet our son for the first time. "Just look at his face; ignore the tubes," I said, quoting the excellent advice someone had given me when heading to see Rafi in the ICU.

Our spiritual and motivational attitude was clear: "Think good, and as a result, it will be good," said the nineteenth-century sage, Rabbi Menachem Mendel of Lubavitch. The idea was not simply to paste Pollyannaish smiles on one's face but to actually influence the Divine flow by recognizing that everything G-d does is truly good.[2] We did our best to apply that to our new child, nicknamed "Little Guy." We joined the doctors' rounds every morning, tried our hardest to pick up the medical lingo, attempted to understand his medical situation, and asked questions and added our thoughts when possible. We spruced up his little corner of the NICU with pictures, Jewish books, and the sounds of Chassidic tunes playing out of a little CD player next to his incubator. "Little Guy" plowed through all his milestones, slowly learning how to breathe on his own, eat and gain weight, and, miraculously, came home three fairly unadventurous months later.

His *bris milah*, the ritual circumcision ceremony held ten days after he came home, was emotional, as we named him Yehuda Refael: "Yehuda," with its Hebrew connotation of "thanks," and "Refael," my brother Rafi's name, meaning "G-d heals."

The next four children who appeared in our world did so thankfully less spectacularly—Shayna, then Naomi, and later, Levi and Menachi. But it was child number six, little Nissi, who would challenge us to our core, show us open miracles that almost defied belief, and bring new meaning to the Rebbe's insistence that hospitals be named "places of healing."

---

2   See the book "Positivity Bias" by Mendel Kalmenson for an extensive review of this subject.

Part I

THE JOURNEY

Chapter 1

Standing on the Tracks

Seattle is known for its dreary winters, and the winter of 2015–2016 was right in line with the average. The short gray days were tinged with chilly air and persistent wet mist; the omnipresent low cloud cover obscured the spectacular skyline of snow-capped mountains and sparkling bodies of water for months on end. One pleads to see the sun—be it even for a few moments.

Despite the dreariness outside, our family's calendar was full. As the co-directors of Chabad at University of Washington, my wife and I had a slew of activities planned to brighten the days and evenings of the Jewish students and faculty. Our Chanukah schedule was jam-packed with events: a public menorah lighting honoring the president of the University; a party for young professionals at a downtown billiard hall—perhaps ironically named "Temple Billiards"; a mobile-menorah parade led by our thirty-four-foot RV "Mitzvah Tank"; and, as a chaplain in the United States Air Force Reserve, a holiday party on base for soldiers and airmen at my home station, Joint Base Lewis-McChord. Our children also had their various school programs, and a little family gathering would round things out. A lot of light, laughter, and hard work looked back at us from our calendar.

Chaya was entering her thirtieth week of a mostly uneventful pregnancy (uneventful, if you exclude the nausea that bedeviled her for a third of that time—par for the course for this mother of five), and as such, she'd be going to the University Hospital midwives for her thirty-week checkup on the morning of the fourth day of Chanukah, prior to our campus menorah lighting.

With all our responsibilities, we split up. I stood outside in the damp cold, meeting students and urging them to come to the program that evening, while distributing tin menorahs and packages of candles to all who needed them. Chaya had several stops to make all over town, including picking up the traditional Chanukah jelly donuts from the bakery, hot coffee from the bagel shop, and festive decorations from the craft store. In between all that and ferrying our four schoolchildren to and from school, she squeezed in the routine appointment with the midwives—expecting it to be over quickly so she could get back to campus with all the supplies and with enough time before the program to help me set up.

But things were no longer straightforward.

She called from the car on her way out of the appointment. "Elie," she said, angst tingeing her voice, "I think there's something wrong with the baby's heart."

CHAYA IS NO VAIN WORRIER. Following the premature birth of Yehuda, our eldest son, we'd been "condemned" to high-risk follow-up for all of her subsequent pregnancies. She hated the high-risk team, finding them unsupportive of our desire to have a large family. The pressure to commit to a particular family planning method would start far before the actual birth of the child, and Chaya felt that detracted significantly from the special joy of bringing a new soul into the world.

It was during this pregnancy that she opted to return to the hospital's midwives, with whom we had started out with Yehuda. Their attitude had been far more supportive—more gentle in both speech and substance. And considering that we had four healthy births since the first, we felt no reason to go back to the gloom and doom of the high-risk world.

The midwives welcomed us back to their practice, some of them even recalling Chaya from eleven years prior. The pregnancy proceeded calmly, until that thirty-week checkup. The midwives had insisted on only one specific ultrasound, which would ascertain the position of the placenta. Mistakenly, an order was placed for a full ultrasound, a complete analysis of the anatomy of the fetus. Things went awry from there.

As the veteran of dozens of ultrasounds from all of her previous "high-risk" pregnancies, Chaya understood very quickly that the technician was spending way too much time around the baby's heart, measuring various angles and taking down all sorts of notes. No information was forthcoming yet. The technician simply said, "A doctor will call you with the results." But as Chaya drove home from the appointment, she confided her worries to me.

We had subtle, inexplicable feelings that we had expressed privately to each other. Very early in the pregnancy, Chaya felt like something would be wrong with the baby. I tried to calm her fears, thinking them baseless. And then, after Yom Kippur that year, as we walked away from our little synagogue on Greek Row, I told her, "I felt that I was fighting something the entire Yom Kippur, but was up against a wall. I feel like I lost a battle." Those fleeting thoughts between the two of us turned out to be somewhat prophetic.

ABOUT AN HOUR BEFORE the campus menorah lighting, the midwife reached me on my cell phone. Chaya had not yet reached campus, still on her pre-program errands, and she was not picking up her phone, so the midwife—somewhat hesitantly—agreed to talk to me. "It looks like the baby has several serious heart defects," she told me. My own heart sank.

Searching for some reassurance, or at least to assess the fight we'd be up against, I responded, "I know you're not a doctor, but based on the information you have, do you think the baby is viable?" She hemmed and hawed, and after being pressed a bit, finally replied, "Look, I'm *not* a doctor, so I don't want to make an authoritative statement. But considering the severity of the malformations, I don't believe so."

"So what's the plan?" I asked as more questions flooded my mind.

"We made your wife an appointment with a fetal cardiologist for next week, and we transferred her care to a high-risk OB-GYN. They will find out more and be able to answer all your questions. Best of luck to you...and I'm sorry..."

"Thanks," I gulped.

I withheld the bad news from Chaya until after the program—an extremely successful one, with some one hundred people in attendance. There was no need for her to try and deal with the bombshell while trying to run a program, meet and greet new and old students alike, and encourage others while trying to keep her own emotions under check. So for the meantime, I kept it under wraps.

The ceremony began, and I stood in front of the expectant crowd, digging deep, trying to give myself the strength for whatever would lie ahead. As the six-foot wooden menorah stood beside me, flames aglow, I stressed the idea that the menorah speaks to us. It tells us that miracles *do* happen, even nowadays. "The blessing we make on the menorah thanks G-d, Who did miracles in those Biblical times and does miracles during our times as well. The menorah stands as testimony that G-d is fully capable of doing what He wants, whether within the laws of nature, using them as a tool to accomplish His Will, or beyond the laws of nature," I said. Truth be told, I was talking to myself as much as I was to the crowd; my extemporaneous speech was, in reality, a personal, internal battle cry.

After the menorah ceremony concluded, the refreshed students scurried back to their final exams, and I privately told Chaya of my devastating conversation with the midwife. Chaya reacted to the news as I had—taking it in quietly, with no visible reaction—and we cleaned up from the program in the darkened silence of the abandoned plaza, our thoughts swirling in the recesses of our own minds.

Winter break now provided us with a calm before the storm to settle upon a strategic game plan. First and foremost, we recognized that our family needed to maintain its stability. We decided to put our student programming and organization building on hold in order to maintain the emotional bandwidth for the fight ahead. And at the center of our hopes and fears, we placed these two ideas: (1) G-d can do anything, and, because of that, (2) think positive.

That second one wasn't easy. Who were we to merit G-d's miracles? And alongside that self-doubt, we faced another challenge. Keeping our minds off the terrible news was hard enough, but when well-meaning people would ask the visibly pregnant Chaya, "Congratulations! When are you due? Do you know the gender of the baby?" the comments and questions stung us with the reminder of the reality we were facing.

A WEEK AFTER THE MENORAH LIGHTING, we were ushered into the hushed offices of prenatal imaging for an in-depth ultrasound and echocardiogram. The technician silently poked and prodded, measured and marked, all the while staring at the static-like images on the screen. Barely a word was uttered. At the conclusion of the three-hour study, the receptionist brought us into a small conference room. Nothing sat in the room besides for a small table, chairs, and a box of tissues. The lack of decor was a teasing contrast to the amount of emotion that the room undoubtedly saw on a regular basis.

We were soon joined by a trio of solemn-faced women: a cardiologist—a woman of apparent Irish descent with short copper hair; an OB-GYN—a slim woman with Asian features; and a blonde Caucasian social worker. The latter took notes copiously, saving us the trouble of trying to comprehend the complex anatomical and medical information being thrown at us. The cardiologist, Dr. Fern, spoke first. All things considered, she had comparatively good news to share with us.

"Your baby has three major malformations of the heart: he only has a right ventricle—his left ventricle is way too small to do anything (unbalanced AV Canal, or single-ventricle defect); his pulmonary artery is stunted (pulmonary atresia); and the pulmonary veins go through his liver, and only then to the heart (infracardiac total anomalous pulmonary venous connection, known as TAPVC). This is a congenital heart disease on the severe end of the spectrum. Considering that this baby has three of the twelve heart defects defined as critical, he will need immediate surgery as soon as he's born to correct the issues. This would be just the first in a series of three operations over his first few years. The first would be the placement of a Blalock-Taussig (BT) Shunt, followed afterward by the Glenn and Fontan heart surgeries, to allow the baby to survive. I cannot guarantee the survival of the baby, as the childhood mortality of this degree of disease is high, but this is the only medical option available. If the baby does not get immediate care within a few hours of his birth, he will not be able to live."

It would take us a while to understand what this meant, but the practical upshot of these complex heart defects was that this baby only had half a heart. And if that weren't bad enough, he really had no functional circulatory system to shuttle blood between his heart and lungs, and by extension, no way to get his blood to absorb the oxygen it needed. The valve to pump blood from the heart to the lungs was a solid mass, instead of the usual operating valve, which opens and closes as the heart beats. And, finally, the veins that carry oxygenated blood from the lungs to the heart were in the wrong place—instead of transiting from the lungs to the heart, they led from the lungs, meandered below the diaphragm and into the liver, and only then to the heart—which could result in catastrophic backup of blood, damaging the lungs. The surgeries mentioned would first create a temporary system of blood flow with the BT Shunt, and later, at about six months of age, with the Glenn, create new "plumbing" for the heart. The Fontan would be the final corrective fix, at about three or four years old.[1]

But to my mind, all this information was a distraction from the immediate good news. Dr. Fern had mentioned that magical word: surgery! The fact that a surgical option was available was, in fact, great news, and gave us a fighting chance. I was ready to jump on it, and I told them so. But Dr. Mothers, the high-risk OB-GYN, spoke up, and she put an immediate damper on things with the information that she provided. "It seems from the ultrasound that there are several other major issues to contend with. The baby also seems to have complications in his esophagus and trachea, what we would refer to as esophageal atresia or esophageal fistula—the esophagus is either stunted or fused with the trachea. We also can't find his stomach in the imaging, so it's possible he has none. And considering all that, on top of the extreme complexity of his heart condition, it's really too much for us to fix surgically." Dr. Mothers paused, with a grim look on her face. "I'm so sorry..."

The severity of the situation now clearly apparent, we walked out of that appointment crushed. We drove home in silence. Pulling into our driveway, we sat in the car for a few minutes. A quiet conversation of shared pain led us to a place of commitment to support each other, first and foremost, and to do whatever we could for this baby.

---

1   See the diagrams of Nissi's heart and each of these surgeries on page 179.

Deep within, we knew that the game wasn't over. The Talmud's exhortation rang in my ears: "Even if an unsheathed sword lies upon your neck, one must never withhold himself from G-d's mercy!"[2]

On the one hand, we felt completely overwhelmed by the magnitude of the issues facing us. Yet we felt absolutely and totally committed to action. So we began a series of plans, medically, as well as spiritually, to try to avert the inevitable, all based upon the advice of the Lubavitcher Rebbe, a man of both spiritual and practical genius, whose inspiration and guidance we live with on a daily basis.

Our first plan of action was to ask that the scans be retaken. The Rebbe noted that internal imaging can occasionally be misread. The team did so, just a few days after the first imaging, but no new information was forthcoming. The diagnoses and prognoses remained the same as they had from the original scans.

We next asked the team if they could refer us to another doctor for a second opinion. Dr. Fern willingly referred us to the pediatric cardiology department at Boston Children's Hospital, one of the top pediatric heart centers in the country. The doctor to whom we were referred, Dr. Snow, had actually been Dr. Fern's mentor, so she readily sent his scans and her team's prognosis to him. Shortly thereafter, we received a response from Dr. Snow: "Considering the complexity of the case, I would agree with the team in Seattle: surgery would be futile." Dr. Snow's staff half-heartedly offered us the opportunity to move to Boston immediately until the birth in two months' time, but Dr. Snow's own unencouraging comments coupled with the seeming impossibility of such an extreme and sudden move for our family caused us to quickly disregard this option.

Back to the drawing board we went. Another piece of the Rebbe's advice for medical situations was to consult "a doctor who is a friend." Considering that, we reached out to a neonatologist, Dr. Ralph, a Jewish doctor who had been involved in Yehuda's care as a preemie. We knew that he worked both in the hospital in which Chaya would give birth,

---

2   *Berachos*, 10a.

University Hospital, as well as in Seattle Children's Hospital, where any procedures would take place. At the time, we mistakenly believed that they were both part of the same hospital system. We hoped Dr. Ralph would be able to provide us with assistance in navigating both hospitals, and perhaps help us find a novel medical way out of our baby's predicament.

Dr. Ralph had always been nice to us, albeit in a professional manner. Over the eleven years that had passed since Yehuda's birth and NICU hospitalization, we had stayed in light contact. But on the rare occasion that we did see each other in person, we embraced like old friends. So it was to him that I turned in my search for an advocate.

"Elie, Elie..." he sighed upon hearing of the multiple malformations, which I rattled off to him as if from a scroll in ancient Latin. "This isn't a conversation for the phone. Let's meet in person." To that, I readily agreed.

Several days later, we got together to discuss things. We sat opposite each other in a quaint neighborhood coffee shop, and Dr. Ralph described to me the formation of the child as it unfolds miraculously in utero. As he did so, he detailed all the defects that had apparently developed in this child, explaining each of them in particular. He explained that the odds were stacked so high against this baby that there really wasn't anything to do. "The cardiac issues are very, very serious," he said. "But the esophageal atresia or fistula compounds issues by an order of magnitude—because in order to fix that, you need a perfectly working heart and lungs. And this baby has critical issues in both of those departments—each individual heart defect that he has is already a major problem, to say nothing of all three. And with the blood flow from his heart severely compromised, his lungs will not function properly, let alone at a high level."

I heard him out, but gently corrected him, based on our mutual previous experiences. "As you well know, with G-d's help, we've beaten the odds before. Your former patient, our former preemie, is now a perfectly healthy eleven-year-old boy. He had very significant odds against him as well—perhaps not as steep as these, but certainly significant nonetheless. And, as religious Jews, of course we believe fully in miracles.

We'd like to take the tack that we're going to expect miracles. Now, what medical approach are we going to take to merit those miracles?"

"Well, I believe in miracles as well," Dr. Ralph agreed. "Otherwise, I would not be practicing medicine; and I certainly remember Yehuda's case well. But in my opinion, there's no comparison. In fact, I would not attempt anything for this child because there is little chance he'll survive the operating table. And even if he does survive that, there is even less chance that he'll survive much longer, and certainly not with any quality of life. I've seen children who have never even seen the outside of the hospital before dying..."

That was irrelevant. I patiently explained to him, as I had to Dr. Fern and Dr. Mothers, that according to Jewish Law and attitude, we are not worried about the quality of life, but of life itself, for every moment of life has infinite value, value that cannot be defined by simple mortal rationale. Instead, if there was any chance whatsoever to save the baby, we were going to take it, no matter the outcome.

I WAS SERIOUS ABOUT THAT. We were absolutely sure what our responsibilities were as parents: do whatever needs to be done to protect this child for as long as he lives because we truly can't place a value on the time that body and soul are together. We cannot possibly comprehend what kinds of spiritual accomplishments, what G-dly purpose, exist in a life, even one in which much of the person's physicality is devoid of opportunity or experiences due to any kind of physical or even mental limitation.

For me, this idea was not academic but very personal. As a teenager, I went through a very intense experience, which gave me an intimate connection with this idea—how even a person whose quality of life (a highly relative and subjective measure, in any case) was diminished still retained purpose and value far beyond the simplistic terms our society deem as qualitative.

It happened during the last days of my brother Rafi's life. Due to an infection in his lungs, he was in a medically induced coma in the ICU at Shadyside Hospital in Pittsburgh, and things were not going well. After a very stressful day, my usually rock-steady parents were in tears, and it broke me to see them in such a state. I went to sleep that night an emotional mess...and awoke the next morning in a surprising state of euphoria. To this day, I remember the first thoughts I had that morning: "Why am I feeling so happy when my brother is in the hospital dying?"

And then, the dream I'd just had came back to me in full color. In it, I found myself at a *farbrengen*, a Chassidic celebration, at Lubavitch Headquarters, with the Rebbe himself. This was in 1997, while the Rebbe's physical presence had left this world three years prior. In my dream, I approached the Rebbe's table, and the Rebbe asked me, "What's wrong?" Noting the tension and grief Rafi's hospitalization was causing our family, I exclaimed, "Rebbe, we can't handle this!" The Rebbe gave me a meaningful look and said, "It'll be better for him in the World to Come..." And then I awoke.

As I reviewed the dream and its message in my head, I came to understand that Rafi's sickness and even incapacitation had a Divine purpose, beyond human rationale. And the Rebbe's words also set me up with the honest realization of what was happening—Rafi passed away a week later.

APPLYING THAT LESSON to the matter at hand, I tried hard to not consider the possibility of our baby living life in a vegetative state. My focus was to protect that baby's body and soul; to allow them to be fused for as long as G-d deemed necessary, with whatever capabilities G-d, in His infinite wisdom, would grant him.

The rationalistic Dr. Ralph listened intently to my words, nodding. I continued my monologue. "Back in the 1850s, the third Lubavitcher Rebbe, Rabbi Menachem Mendel of Lubavitch, taught a profound thought. Quoting the Talmudic statement[3] that doctors have been given permission by G-d to heal, he added, 'But not to cause hopelessness with predictions.' Let's focus on the healing element, and leave the future to G-d."

In Ralph's response, it seemed that he understood what I was saying, even though he may have disagreed with some of it. Given that, I asked

---

3   *Berachos* 60a.

him to take a look at the scans himself. Perhaps he would see something that the other doctors had not, which might lead us to a different, and more optimistic, approach. He replied that he needed my permission to access our case files, and I willingly gave it, asking him to be our advocate, to which he agreed. Happy and appreciative to have an ally, we parted with a handshake and a hug.

I never could have imagined where his "advocacy" would lead us.

THE HEAVINESS OF OUR SITUATION was exacerbated by the now-weekly high-risk OB visits, which were worse than ever. A social worker joined the OB-GYN at each appointment. (Ironically, this social worker was not only Jewish, but had attended a *shabbaton* weekend that we had co-sponsored with our Chabad on Campus colleagues of her alma mater many years earlier.) Young and inexperienced, she tried her best to apply her recently acquired education on us, using textbook methodology. Toward the end of each session, she'd ask us in a mournful tone, "So have you decided how you would like the baby's last moments to be enacted? Do you have any plans for the funeral?"

We explained to her that the Jewish approach was not to focus on death until it happened. She couldn't seem to comprehend that idea, and asked, attempting the old psychological manipulation: "Well, would you like me to call the local Jewish Burial Society, or would you like to call them?" I spat back, "If you'd like to talk to the gravediggers, you're welcome to do so on your own behalf, not on ours!"

This ridiculous conversation repeated itself in various mutations over numerous visits as I tried my hardest to explain how Judaism is life-obsessed, not death-obsessed. "We call a cemetery a *beis hachayim*, a 'house of life.' We refer to death as 'life after life.' I don't want to, or feel it necessary at all, to focus on the death of the baby while we're still waiting for him to be born! What happens later can be dealt with later," I told them. But despite the nodding heads, I was speaking to deaf ears—and minds.

At the end of each such appointment, with the medical situation unchanged but the baby in utero apparently stable, I would conclude with desperate hope, "But we expect miracles!" And the doctors and the social worker would shake their heads sympathetically, their eyes and expressions saying, "These poor, deluded parents; they have no clue what's about to hit them." It would take us days to recover emotionally from these consultations. We certainly had more than just a clue what was going on, but we had an approach determined by Judaism and Chassidic philosophy that was directing us, and we were going to stick with that until the end.

During this deep, dark period, we were being pressed constantly by both the high-risk doctor and social worker, and later by Dr. Ralph, to "plan out the baby's last moments," at least for the sake of the birth team. I refused to do so for several weeks, but the pressure didn't relent, so I finally agreed to have a "theoretical conversation." We understood the dim prognosis well, but we wanted to maintain a spiritual focus on positivity to keep that possible channel open. Introducing a "death plan" felt like giving up, and that just does not exist in our Jewish playbook. But I eventually agreed to make a plan for the simple reason that I wanted to resolve any issues of Jewish law (halachah) in advance, to ensure we fulfilled our religious, ethical, and spiritual responsibilities for this child to a tee, no matter what would happen.

To do so, I arranged a meeting between our local halachic authority, Rabbi Mordechai Farkash, and Dr. Ralph. The two met at my house, and I seated them comfortably on the couches in our living room. Ralph parried all questions as he patiently explained to Rabbi Farkash that the prenatal scans were virtually definitive, and that there was but a fractional chance that the baby would survive up to and through the first surgery. It was for that reason that he suggested that a noninvasive course of action be taken—allow the baby to be born and die, without intensive and pointless attempts at saving him.

Rabbi Farkash challenged the doctor from various angles—how could he be absolutely certain? But Ralph was resolute in his conviction regarding the finality of the prognosis. "Chances are very high that the baby will not survive birth at all; after all, the heart defects he has should prevent him from breathing. Even if he does survive birth, he will probably die during any testing that we'd do following birth. If he manages to get through that, there is no way that he'll be able to survive transportation from the University Hospital labor and delivery ward via ambulance to Seattle Children's Hospital, where any surgery would be performed. And if he manages to survive *that*, he will certainly die on the operating table. And if, somehow, he doesn't die then, he'll definitely be a vegetable until he dies soon after."

Based on that no-holds-barred information, Rabbi Farkash sadly responded, "So you're saying that medically speaking, there is absolutely nothing that you can do for this baby?" Dr. Ralph concurred emphatically. Rabbi Farkash said slowly, "Well, if there's nothing you can do, then there's no option, and no point in 'heroically' doing surgery with no healing purpose in mind. However, the one thing you need to know is this: according to Torah law, nutrition and air must not be withheld. If the baby is put on oxygen, he may not be taken off, and he must be fed."

I took in this information and interjected. "I hear you, and I understand where things stand. You've been asking for a birth plan, and here's what I want: I would like the birth to take place *as if* there is a chance to save his life. As soon as this baby is born, I'd like to retake any scans, to ensure that we have any and all data possible. That way, if there ends up being any chance whatsoever that we can get him into surgery and save his life, we're going to take it."

Dr. Ralph agreed energetically. "Oh, we can do that! We will induce your wife a little early, at 39 weeks. As soon as the baby is born, if he is alive, we can give him prostaglandin. That's a drug to keep his patent ductus arteriosus, the small hole between the heart and the lungs known as the PDA, open. The PDA would otherwise close within hours of birth, making it impossible for the baby to shuttle blood between his lungs and heart, killing him almost immediately. We will have a top-level team of radiologists on hand to read the scans immediately." That sounded good to me, so the plan was finalized. Any information that could lead to a chance at saving the baby's life would be utilized.

Parallel to these physical preparations, our spiritual warfare had already begun in earnest, and we intensified it as much as we could. The Rebbe often told people in crisis to check the scrolls in their tefillin and mezuzahs to make sure they were still kosher, as according to Jewish mysticism, both have protective qualities. So we did so. We sent our mezuzahs off to New York to be checked by competent scribes and arranged for a videoed walk-through of our house with a scribe to ensure that their placement on our doors was correct. In fact, we found four misplaced mezuzahs, which were promptly corrected. We also replaced a number of mezuzahs that were of inferior quality with mezuzahs of a higher standard, and bought the highest-quality mezuzahs for the external doors of our house.

Shockingly, one mezuzah, which was on a door that was not required to have a mezuzah in the first place, was found to have two ominous, invalidating mistakes—in the words *"levavechem"* and *"b'neichem,"* meaning "your heart" and "your son."

We were sure that these corrective measures would have an impact, and were therefore deeply disappointed when we received Dr. Snow's e-mail from Boston Children's Hospital, stating that this baby had too many defects to correct, and that any operative measures would be, in his words, "futile."

THE WEEKS PASSED INEXORABLY. We grimly set ourselves toward the future, taking our keys from the biblical patriarch Jacob: prayer, hoping for the best, but also preparing ourselves for the worst.[4]

My father, as the father of a child with cystic fibrosis and therefore no stranger to medical crises himself, shared a thought to keep me afloat during this difficult period: For a long time, scientists had described a certain crystal found on tooth enamel as having six sides. This was a "fact" taught for decades, until a new microscope revealed that they were actually looking at the crystal *and its shadow*! The crystal really only had *four* sides.[5] So, he emphatically pointed out, the scans can be wrong!

I, in my darkness, and despite all my efforts to remain positive, thought to myself, *fat chance.* But still, it was enough to buoy my spirits a little, so I put the information on a back shelf in my mind. After all,

---

4   Genesis 32:8.
5   See https://www.chabad.org/library/article_cdo/aid/2531/jewish/Reality-and-Its-Shadow.htm.

we were absolutely sure miracles *could* happen...but *would* miracles possibly happen for us? We felt there was no way we would ever be worthy of Divine intervention to the degree we needed...

The spiritual combat continued. Our friends at Chabad on Campus International graciously sponsored a flight to visit the Rebbe's gravesite, where I laid everything on the Rebbe's broad shoulders, asking him to intercede on our behalf to G-d. The brief visit—less than twenty-four hours to fly cross-country and back—was mentally, emotionally, and spiritually therapeutic.

As I was leaving the synagogue outside the cemetery, I noticed a video of the Rebbe playing on the screen at the entrance to the Visitor's Center. In the video, the Rebbe spoke about the significance of the arboreal holiday, Tu B'Shevat. He explained elements of the metaphor that man is compared to a tree, as in the verse, "For man is a tree of the field."[6] Said the Rebbe, "It's not enough to be any tree; one must be a fruit tree, providing sustenance to others." A quiet, optimistic message sank into my weary brain: *Whatever we are going through, will, in the end, be "fruitful." Whatever happens has a Divine purpose.*

ODDLY ENOUGH, while we were undergoing all this, we were also preparing for a family celebration: our son Menachi's third birthday and first haircut, his *upsherenish*. There was a brief moment when we considered having a more toned-down affair instead of the festive open-house celebration we'd thrown for his older brothers, Yehuda and Levi. But upon considering the Rebbe's approach to maintain positivity—and even project joy—alongside the fact that we did not want our children to lose out on any elements of celebrating Judaism due to anything beyond their control, we decided to continue with the party as if nothing else was going on. In fact, it ended up being a beautiful celebration with family and friends, and gave us a reprieve from the darkness we were wading through.

Menachi's birthday is on the Hebrew date 10 Shevat, which is also the anniversary of the passing of the previous Lubavitcher Rebbe, Rabbi

---

6   Deuteronomy 20:19.

Yosef Yitzchak Schneerson. Considering the auspiciousness of the day, I undertook to bring in a speaker to speak to the community at our home and Chabad House toward the end of the celebration. And indeed, after the party, we held a spirited Chassidic gathering with Rabbi Michoel Seligson, a scholar of note whose father had been the Rebbe's in-house go-to doctor.

At some point during the *farbrengen*, I took the floor. I described our unborn son's situation in as vague terms as possible, and attempted to learn spiritual lessons from the various aspects of the illnesses he'd been diagnosed with, in desperate imitation of several stories told in the *Zohar*[7] and Chassidic tradition. Addressing his heart defects, I noted the importance of having a complete heart, that even the "left" side—the side that metaphorically represents our animal soul—is an important part of a healthy person. I also spoke about the importance of internalizing spiritual "food": how Torah needs to permeate a person the same way food is broken down and nutrition is extracted, becoming part of your very self.

Everyone wished a hearty *l'chayim* that everything should turn out well, recalling the Chassidic aphorism, "What a Chassidic *farbrengen* can accomplish, even the angel Michael cannot."[8] A friend, Mendel Notik, pulled out one hundred dollars in single bills and passed them around the table with a charity box, and all the participants gave charity in the merit of the unborn child. The *farbrengen* ended on those notes of prayerful hope.

Around that time, a close friend and fellow Chabad emissary, Rabbi Shimon Emlen, was blessed with a baby boy, and he and his wife decided to give me the honor of being *sandek*, holding the baby at his *bris milah*. Knowing that there is a deep spiritual significance in the honor, I accepted, all the while praying that the happy and auspicious occasion somehow have an impact on our own unborn baby.

---

7   See *Zohar, Balak*, 204a.

8   *Hayom Yom*, 26 Kislev.

A FINAL EVENT OCCURRED during those awful weeks of waiting that was to have a huge impact on the proceedings as they went along. Prior to the prenatal diagnosis, Chaya had planned to spend part of her spring break in Los Angeles with several of her friends and colleagues from the Chabad on Campus network. Now, she regrettably informed them that she would not be able to join them, as she was stuck at home due to the grim situation and doctor's orders instructing her not to travel. But the women didn't hesitate, responding instead by asking, "So why don't we come to you?"

The four friends flew out to Seattle from their homes across the West Coast and spent a few days together in laughter and tears. One of these women was a high school friend of Chaya's, Chaya Shapiro. When she returned to her home in Flagstaff, Arizona, she turned to her husband and said, "Dovie, we must do something for them!" (We only learned many years later that Chaya's own mother has congenital heart disease, and her life and the lives of her children were saved by the advice and prayers of the Lubavitcher Rebbe.[9])

Rabbi Dovie Shapiro looked at his wife incredulously. "What would you like to do? What *can* we do?" In desperation, Chaya blurted out, "Let's raise money for them..." Chabad Houses on Campus around the world are self-funded organizations, so for any of us, such assistance from an external source is greatly appreciated.

Dovie and his cousin, Rabbi Avremel Chazanow, undertook a fund-raising project for us, starting with a modest goal of ten thousand dollars. When the match-a-thon went live—and by unbelievable Divine Providence it was unknowingly scheduled for the day that Chaya would be induced—it seemed that the entire Chabad world chipped in. All told, they raised some sixty thousand dollars, which took a massive load off our shoulders. That gift—the gift of freedom from financial worry during the upcoming difficult months—cannot be underestimated. Their campaign also alerted the world about our circumstances, and

---

9   Her incredible story was published by Jewish Educational Media, "Here's My Story," July 1, 2020: http://myencounterblog.com/?p=3835#more-3835.

suddenly, thousands of people across the globe began to pray for our unborn baby by reciting *Tehillim*, the powerful words of Psalms.

A glimmer of hope began to flicker out of the gloom.

Chapter 2

Alive in the Mourning

Time moved along against our will, and the date for the induction eventually arrived. My parents-in-law flew to Seattle from Cincinnati to lend a hand for the next few weeks. Early Sunday evening, on February seventh, Chaya's mother drove us to University Hospital to begin the process of being induced. We entered the hospital heavily. Chaya was thirty-nine weeks into the pregnancy. Very little sleep was to be had that night; Chaya tossed and turned on the medical bed, and I did the same on a cot near her.

When morning dawned, the medical staff began to work in earnest. So did my recital of *Tehillim*. Its words of prayer took on a life I had never known before. Every mention of the words "heart" and "life" became invigorated with an entirely new, deeply personal meaning. King David's pleas for life reverberated quietly in the room. When I arrived at the words of the traditional prayer recited following each book of *Tehillim* that mention a birthing mother, I felt myself shaken to the very core. G-d, I screamed silently, *this isn't some anonymous birthing mother—this is my wife and my unborn son!*

On Monday, February 8, at 12:47 p.m., Nesanel Estrin was born.

Nesanel—the name is made up of the Hebrew words for "G-d gives." That name said it all, and was chosen with deep purpose in mind. In instances of, G-d forbid, stillbirth, the standard Jewish custom is for the *chevrah kaddisha* (the Jewish burial society) to name the child, hoping to take elements of grief away from the parents, but that did not appeal to us at all. Rabbis told us there was nothing wrong with us choosing a name for the child, so we began considering ideas. Chaya had come up with the name Nesanel several weeks prior to his birth. As she put it, "I want his name to indicate our desire to recognize and feel that whatever happens, for however long he lives, was given to us from G-d." Later, Rabbi Farkash told us that it was perfectly permissible to start calling him a name immediately, even though a *bris milah*, the time of the typical baby-naming ceremony, was not exactly on the horizon.

AS THE MEDICAL STAFF worked strenuously, gentle singing could be heard coming from an iPad placed unobtrusively on a shelf. The songs being played came from the *"Niggunei Hisva'adus"* albums, a collection of moments taken directly from the Rebbe's *farbrengens*, in which the Rebbe himself joined the singing. This was my small attempt to instill a calming, spiritual feeling into the room. As Nesanel entered the world, a special tune was heard playing in the background: Shamil's Niggun, as it was sung alone by the Rebbe himself. Shamil's Niggun is one of fourteen tunes that the Rebbe personally taught his disciples. The Rebbe elaborated about its meaning, explaining that its melancholic melody represents the journey of a soul into the body. Hearing the Rebbe's voice sing the sweet strains of that particular soulful song at the moment the baby was born caused my hair to stand on end.

To everyone's surprise, as soon as the baby came out, we heard a raspy but unmistakably vigorous cry. The thought *"That's a good sign"* crossed my addled mind.

Dr. Ralph quickly stabilized the baby, suctioning him and injecting him with prostaglandin, and passed him over to the X-ray and echocardiogram team. As per the birth plan, the team ran the same tests that were given prenatally to determine the degree and type of defects our baby had. While his color was fairly blue, he apparently needed very little oxygen support. His oxygen saturation percentages—known colloquially as "sats"—fluctuated in the 70s and 80s, and sometimes dipped into the 60s. From our preemie experience, we knew numbers that low should set off alarms continuously—after all, healthy people have oxygen sats in the upper 90s—so we watched them with abject fear. Soon, the flurry of activity halted, and we were left to hold our beautiful, but purple, baby boy.

At about 2:30 p.m., Dr. Ralph returned to the room. We looked up at him, expecting to hear some good news, but our anticipation was shattered as he informed us that the original diagnosis was correct. "This baby will not survive to see sunset," he grimly stated, pointing out that the baby's oxygen saturation rates were dropping. These thoughts raced vigorously through my head as I looked at my son: "*C'mon, kid! Make it past sunset. Show this doctor that he isn't G-d! 'Doctors have permission to heal; not to predict!'*" I was also internally hoping that if he'd make it into the next Hebrew date, he'd have some spiritual assistance from the power of the month of Adar—a month that our Sages say has "a healthy luck."[1] In addition, the letters that make up the word Adar can be seen as an acronym for the verse, "I, G-d, am your Healer."[2]

Dr. Ralph once again morbidly described the final minutes of a dying baby and unhooked Nissi from the nasal prongs providing a steady flow of oxygen directly through the baby's nostrils. As he did, Chaya muttered, "What a roller coaster!" Dr. Ralph looked up at the two of us, saying, "No. A roller coaster has ups as well as downs. I'm afraid this situation doesn't have any ups." With those "encouraging" words, he left us to be once again by ourselves.

Unlike with any of our other newborns, Chaya held this baby almost constantly, occasionally handing him to me to get a rest. The baby remained calm, so much so that I asked the nurse if this was usual for such babies. She shook her head no. Luckily for us, he was just an easy baby. Despite his dusky color, he didn't seem to have laborious breathing or any other struggles. Every so often, with any deepening of his color, we would massage his entire body. Each minute passed, second by agonizing second, and I continued whispering the words of *Tehillim*.

WHAT DO YOU DO for a child apparently only meant to be in this world for a few short hours? As I mentioned earlier, Chassidic philosophy teaches about the infinite value of every moment that a body and soul are together. The soul, being a veritable part of G-d, has a purpose in

---

1   *Taanis* 29b.
2   Exodus 15:26.

this world beyond human comprehension. Its ultimate purpose can only be fulfilled when fused with a physical body, its exact mission a Divine secret. It's not our job to define one's purpose, but to support the union of body and soul, in whatever shape it takes, for as long as it lasts.

Chaya and I were both raised on the philosophy of these ideas, infused with stories that taught these lessons, and now we had the daunting task to apply them to our own son. We desperately tried to channel that, attempting to maximize every moment of his precious life, despite our unfathomable sadness. We sang quietly to him, spoke to him, and prayed, trying to fill those moments with love and whatever spirituality we could pull out of our own exhausted and shattered souls.

The minutes passed in the stillness of those quiet moments. We took turns holding him, watching his every breath anxiously. As we got to know our little Nesanel, we deliberately chose the nickname "Nissi," Hebrew for "my miracle." Whenever any of the medical staff would ask his name, we'd say, with desperate hope in our hearts, "His name is 'Nissi,' which means 'my miracle,' because that's what we're praying for." If only he'd be somehow found worthy of one...

At about 4:30 p.m., just after the beginning of sunset, we began noticing the baby's color was starting to look a little less dusky, eventually turning a ruddy pink. All this while, he vigorously chomped a pacifier, with a suck that was strong and firm. (A nurse had to sneak that pacifier to us, as the University Hospital is a certified breastfeeding center, and as such, they do not allow pacifiers in the labor and delivery ward!) Sunset came and went...and Nissi was clearly still alive.

At about 6:00 p.m., with the baby looking as well as could possibly be imagined, we thought perhaps we should be pursuing some sort of care. After all, things seemed to be going far better than the original prediction of "he won't make it to sunset!" In addition, Dr. Fern had given us a four- to six-hour window to get him into surgery, and we were fast approaching that deadline.

We called the nurse and asked her to bring a doctor, preferably a cardiologist, to analyze the situation. Instead of calling a doctor, she summoned a NICU nurse and the NICU charge nurse, and we tried to get them onto our—hopeful—side.

From this point onward, we found ourselves trying to straddle the line between recognizing and accepting the severity of the situation, but at the same time looking for cracks in the diagnosis that could somehow save our son. As we communicated with the team, we tried desperately not to sound irrational or grief-stricken.

We pleaded with them to reassess things, given Nissi's seeming strength. But the NICU charge nurse had all the sensitivity of a rock, actively discouraging us from doing anything. In a condescending tone, she snapped, "There is really nothing else to do that hasn't been done. If you want to go to the Surgical Center at Seattle Children's, you need to leave right now. But all they will do there is repeat the same tests we did earlier today, and get the same results, so I don't know why you want to do that." I refused to give up, saying, "I'm not talking as a grieving parent. Look at the kid from a clinical point of view! Obviously, you got something wrong, because he's still alive and doing fine!" But my pleas were met with the empty looks of false sympathy.

Still, I asked for a cardiologist such as Dr. Fern to be called. Instead, we were informed that Dr. Ralph would be returning to talk to us once again. It was at this point that I began to feel that something was wrong with his approach. Was it an ego trip that he was on, causing him to delight in playing G-d? With little choice in the matter in any case, we decided to allow him to come back and see what he had to say.

Dr. Ralph apologized for his previous prediction of four to six hours but insisted that the baby would not survive long. "Sometimes these things take longer than we expect," he said morbidly. I shot back, "Yeah, sometimes they take seventy or eighty years!"

I asked him to speak to the surgical team at Seattle Children's Hospital to find out if there were any new options, given the baby's evident strength. With a note of resignation, he replied, "There are two surgeons at Seattle Children's. One is a mechanic and will operate on *anything*. There's another who is the one I trust. I'll speak to him." With that reassurance, he left.

We heard Dr. Ralph's words, but something just didn't sit well. The clinical situation didn't match up to the prognosis. It seemed evident that some element of the diagnosis had been incorrect, but no one was willing to admit it. We were desperate for an authentic ally who could help us differentiate between unrealistic hope coming from a place of grief and an honest assessment of Nissi's medical situation.

In the hope that perhaps an outsider would provide some clarity, we called a friend who is a pediatrician and asked if she could swing by. A little later she entered the room with hot dinner. She wished us a bittersweet mazel tov, but when we asked for her medical opinion on his condition and what we should do, she sadly demurred. "This baby's complexity is completely beyond my expertise." It seemed like we had struck out yet again.

CONSIDERING HIS GASTROINTESTINAL ANATOMY was assumed to be dysfunctional, Nissi was not being fed. But that evening, remembering Rabbi Farkash's instructions not to starve the baby, I asked the nurse what would be done regarding feeding him. "Perhaps he could be connected to an IV to make sure he has some kind of nutrition even if we're unsure of his stomach anatomy?" I suggested. The nurse assured us that the baby had enough fat reserves for twenty-four hours, and if the baby would survive that long, the doctors would review the situation. I retorted, "At 12:00 tomorrow, we're getting him onto an IV—stomach or not!"

Well into the middle of the night, the baby had a bowel movement, and we cautiously asked if that proved that he, in fact, had a functioning digestive system. The nurse (erroneously) replied that it did not prove anything, only that he had a functioning intestine. When the baby's diaper was changed, the nurse decided to give the baby his first bath and get his weight—this was at about 2:00 a.m., some thirteen hours after the baby was born. (Truth be told, we had been asked if we wanted him bathed after the post-birth tests, but at the time, given the grim prognosis that baby had only a matter of hours if not minutes in him, we opted to hold him instead.)

We tried to settle down for some semblance of sleep, but sleep was hard to come by, for the third night in a row. And sometime in the wee hours of the morning, Chaya awoke up from a terrifying dream. In her nightmare, Dr. Ralph had grabbed the baby from her and was running away with him, down the hallway of the hospital. Chaya awoke with a start, and, tears streaming down her face, pulled Nissi close in a protective embrace.

THE DAY DAWNED, and as it was Rosh Chodesh Adar, the beginning of the new month, the extra prayers granted me greater chances to plead with G-d for assistance. I sang through all of the praises of *Hallel* in the same manner that I do at the Passover Seder, inserting songs in every paragraph, while holding the baby tight. As I sang, I came upon a sentence that I had said so many times, but never quite internalized: "I shall not die, for I shall live, and I shall tell of G-d's handiwork! G-d has indeed punished me, but not put me to death."[3] The newfound meaning and relevance in this humble expression caused me to tremble with emotion.

At midday, we aggressively revisited the question of feeding the baby. But once again, instead of exploring that option, the nurses responded that Dr. Ralph would be coming soon to discuss things. Frustration began to build—why were we continuously seeing the same doomsayer? Where were the other doctors? And why were we not seeing them? In the meantime, Nissi was not being fed at all.

Finally, at about 1:30 p.m., Dr. Ralph entered the room and sat down next to us. I inquired, "Did you ask the surgeon if he'd take on the case?" He quietly answered that he had, but the surgeon—and by extension, Seattle Children's Hospital—refused to operate, given the gravity of his case.

Little did we know, at the very same time, Seattle Children's Hospital had us on their "Stork List" of babies to be rushed into surgery (due to our prenatal visits with Dr. Fern), and were waiting for us. Completely unbeknownst to us, Dr. Ralph had taken things into his own hands and told them that we refused surgery and opted instead for palliative care.

But then he told us the very best news we had heard in months. Sticking to his guns, he prefaced it with negativity. He spoke in an exaggerated whisper, demonstrating pretended pain, until Chaya,

---

3   *Tehillim* 118:17–18.

annoyed and seeing through his façade, said to him sharply, "Speak louder! I can't hear you!" Clearing his throat, he raised his voice to normal conversation levels. "When I originally spoke to you, I told you that this type of disease often comes with even more problems than we thought..." But after dragging us through that mud, he finally said, "One of the things the tests yesterday revealed is that it seems the baby has a very rare condition called heterotaxy syndrome. This means that his internal organs are flipped, or doubled, or any combination of those two.[4] In this case, this baby has two right sides. For instance, instead of having two lobes on his left lung and three lobes on his right lung, he has three on both. As such, he has a unique internal anatomy, and he *might* have a stomach. It is possible that you might be able to feed him. He also might choke; we don't know. But if you'd like to try to feed him, go ahead."

He warned us that because of heterotaxy syndrome, the baby probably had malrotated intestines, which would swivel the wrong way internally, and therefore might not be able to handle the food. (In fact, the baby's intestines were later proven to be properly formed.) We again tried to argue that the baby was looking great; how could there be no surgical option? But Dr. Ralph was a closed book. In his opinion, nothing could be done.

When he finally left the room, we proceeded to feed the baby sugar water using a syringe, which Nissi eagerly and effortlessly ate. Later that day, the syringe was replaced by a binky trainer, a pacifier attached to a syringe. He sucked on the pacifier and drew food out of the syringe. This method is used to teach feeding to babies who struggle with eating. Nissi quickly proved adept at using it, and soon he was upgraded to drinking baby formula. Over the next few days, he slowly built up his strength, and by the afternoon of February 10, he was eating as much as thirty-five milliliters per feeding from a bottle every two hours, with no choking or spitting up whatsoever. Yet despite all the clinical evidence,

---

4   We'd later hear the joking definition of heterotaxy: throw one hundred internal birth defects into a hat, and the family gets to pick ten at random.

the medical team seemed unmoved. In their view, this baby was simply not supposed to survive.

ALL THIS TIME, we were singularly focused on our deathly ill baby, but we had not completely forgotten about our other five children. In fact, we needed to figure out how to let them in on what was going on without overly traumatizing them.

Before the baby was born, we had reached out to numerous professionals to get advice on dealing with children and loss. Based on those conversations and our own intuition centered on what we felt was best for our family, we didn't plan on having the children meet their new brother only to have him taken from them a short time later. We felt that the emotional connection they'd establish with their brother would cause greater trauma than if they never met him in the first place. Therefore, the original strategy was to inform our other children of the baby's birth only after his passing; but thankfully, Nissi wasn't going along with that plan. Now we were operating somewhat on the fly, with the long-distance direction of the professionals from Chai Lifeline, a superb organization dedicated to helping families of children with severe medical and special needs.

It had become our custom to buy a gift for the older children "from the new baby," and we did the same this time, but with a bit more urgency. In a glimmer of Providence, a few weeks before his birth, we happened upon a once-in-a-lifetime sale at Target: a gaggle of scooters for a few bucks each, and a foosball/pool table combo for an extremely affordable price as well.

I left the hospital to go home that afternoon and bring the kids somewhat up to speed. I told them that their mom had given birth to a new baby brother, and at the same time, I had my parents-in-law, who were babysitting, give them their new toys.

As the kids were happily testing out their new scooters, I prepared myself for the heart-wrenching talks no one ever wants to have. First, I took aside eleven-year-old Yehuda, and then afterward nine-year-old Shayna. I separately told them a well-known story of the founder of the Chassidic movement, Rabbi Israel Baal Shem Tov: He once gave a blessing to a childless couple, who were granted their fervent wish for a baby boy. Sadly, the child passed away just after his third birthday. The distraught couple came back to the Baal Shem Tov, who explained to them that their son was a special soul who had come back into the world for a short time following a full and complete life in order to rectify a slight spiritual defect so that he could ascend to even higher spiritual realms. I looked at their confused faces, and said, "Some souls come into this world for just a short time, and only G-d knows why..." At that last statement, their mouths dropped, and even the normally stalwart Shayna began to cry. I hugged them tight; there were no words to say.

I gave up after speaking to those two—I just couldn't bring myself to have the same conversation with little eight-year-old Naomi, let alone six-year-old Levi and three-year-old Menachi. With a heavy heart, I left my mother-in-law to clean up the mess of the sobbing children and headed back to the hospital.

ON WEDNESDAY, our third day in the hospital, we were visited by Dr. Hitti, one of Chaya's previous high-risk gynecologists. She suggested that Chaya get out of the bed and go for a walk. After all, Chaya hadn't left the room since Sunday night. Chaya asked if she could take the baby along. "Sure," Dr. Hitti said. "You just won't be able to leave the maternity ward because of his security anklet."

Chaya looked at the dozing baby. "But he doesn't have one," she said simply. Dr. Hitti was visibly shocked. Without another word, she marched out to find out why the baby was not given a security anklet.

The nurse came back a few minutes later and strapped the little alarm on his leg. Offhandedly, she remarked, "He actually had not been admitted as a patient to the hospital until now." Apparently, from the hospital's perspective—a perspective directed by Dr. Ralph's medical assessment—it would be easier to record this baby as one who died in hospice. Why unnecessarily complicate things by admitting him as a patient when he was going to die soon enough anyway?

Later that day, we were visited by hospice care nurses, who came by to introduce themselves and enroll us in their "program." Their bright smiles and bouncy demeanor were absurd, considering the circumstances. We had no interest in hospice care, not in the hospital or in our home, and expressed that clearly. "We want to celebrate the life that we have in front of us, not focus on a death that has not yet happened," I endeavored to explain. But like the social worker before them, I could have been speaking gibberish. They simply didn't get what I was saying and continued to proffer forms and brochures. In my eyes, they represented the Angel of Death, despite their smiling faces. After about forty-five minutes, I encouraged them to leave, as the conversation was proving to be exceedingly frustrating. "My wife needs to rest, so if you don't mind, the door is that way…" They finally got the point and left the room, their enrollment papers still unsigned.

Even after their exit, we were still being actively encouraged by the medical staff to leave the hospital that same day, to go home with the baby registered in hospice. Chaya found the thought extremely distressing. How could we just return home to our five other children, to let them see the baby die?! Seeing we weren't moving too quickly, yet wanting us out of the Labor and Delivery Ward, Dr. Ralph arranged for us to be transferred to a room in the NICU, under the pretext of needing feeding help. As evening fell, our belongings were packed up, and we were assisted to move across the hospital to the NICU.

The nurse who brought us there had been with us in the Labor and Delivery ward the previous three days. I noticed that she spent extra time getting Chaya comfortable, fluffing the pillows and fussing around. After a few long moments, she finally looked up, and with a tearstained face, embraced Chaya and whispered, "I just have one thing to say that everyone seems to forget in these circumstances: congratulations on your new baby; he's beautiful." The humanity of that moment was powerful, and we felt somewhat uplifted, despite ourselves.

However, the NICU room we now found ourselves in was like a jail cell. It was placed in the center aisle of the hallway, with no outdoor view, nor any privacy whatsoever. Just the hustle and bustle of the medical teams could be seen and felt outside its glass windows and doors. The windows had shades that could be controlled from either side of the wall, so we played a game of "Open, Shut Them" with the nurses. We'd open the shades to relieve the claustrophobia of the tiny room, and they'd shut them, blocking our view of anything going on in the hallway and giving us the feeling of being trapped in a cardboard box.

In the NICU, Nissi was hooked up just to an oxygen saturation monitor, and nothing else. During our entire time there, we were visited once by the feeding consultant, who pronounced him a proficient eater (not as if we couldn't see that ourselves), and once by Dr. Ralph. No other medical care was given. When Ralph came, he placed his stethoscope on Nissi's chest and listened intently. I asked anxiously, "How does he sound?" To my disgust, Ralph responded by mimicking the gurgling sounds of the stomach. He evidently thought we were idiots.

But positivity briefly entered the room when, to our surprise, the nurse that evening introduced herself. "Hi! My name is Dina," she said brightly. "Do you know Jack Haddash?" We gaped in shock—of course we knew Jack! He was a former student at the University of Washington and had become religiously observant in our home. He had spent the better part of all four years of college at our house, coming to us virtually every Shabbos. "Well," she said, smiling, "he's my brother!" Always searching for the greater purpose of our existence, we jumped on this opportunity. Was she the reason we were going through all this?

We spoke with Dina about our approach—the Jewish approach—regarding celebrating life itself, about the value Judaism places on each individual moment of life, and the frustration that no medical care was being offered. She sympathized, but it seemed clear to us that her hands were tied. Still, her sunny presence and the undeniable Providence that made her our nurse provided us with a bit of a boost.

By this time, Nissi's siblings were itching to meet their new baby brother for the first time, so my father-in-law brought them to the hospital, meeting us in the waiting room of the NICU. Their visit was brief, not more than twenty minutes, as their jittery parents spent most of that time nervously watching the baby's every breath, and then the children were herded back home.

Evening fell, and Chaya and I once again attempted to settle down for a very uneasy night. Having nowhere to go and nothing to do, we just stared at the oxygen saturation monitor. The numbers upon it dropped and climbed with crazy abandon. We would later learn that for a kid with one ventricle, Nissi's oxygen sats had been exactly where they should have been—generally hanging out in the 70s and 80s. Boy, it would have been nice to know that then! All we knew at that point was that he was deathly ill, and his life was hanging by a thread. Eventually, we even disconnected the monitor from him, as it was causing more stress than relevant information. There was nothing we could do about the continuously unstable numbers in any case. It wasn't as if we had nurses or doctors to call if things got too bad, as had been the case when Yehuda had been in the NICU. We really were on our own. The nurses were perfunctory and gave us no medical assistance whatsoever. It was surreal, as if we were stranded on an island surrounded by fresh water yet being prevented from slaking our thirst...

By the morning, we realized that there was nothing left for us in this hospital—or was it a prison? Whatever it was, we needed to get out. Maybe afterward we'd find the strength to reassess things and figure out what our next steps would be.

When we had first been admitted to the NICU, we had been assured by the staff that we would be able to leave whenever we were ready. So at nine o'clock on Thursday morning, we informed the NICU that we were ready to go—we wanted to be discharged from the hospital. But instead of being given the discharge papers, we were in for an absurd series of conversations. First, we were told that we could not leave without being released by Dr. Ralph. He was at a hospital in Tacoma, Washington, over an hour's drive away without traffic. We refused to wait until he arrived. But we were told that he was making his way to us in any case and would be back in Seattle by noon. We had absolutely no interest in seeing him, so we pressed the charge nurse, Mae, to let us go.

Mae then told us that we had to sign into hospice care because otherwise we'd be put under police investigation when the baby died. Being presented with that option, we hesitatingly agreed, but on the condition that the hospice nurse do nothing but sign the papers, without any further conversation. We needed nor wanted any "help" from them.

We were then proffered morphine, telling us that it would come in handy for the baby's final moments. I was stunned by the offer and refused the morphine emphatically. "You haven't trained me to use it; I can kill him with it! In addition, we were told this type of death is painless. And besides, I have children at home, and I don't want a heavy drug in my house for no reason. I'm not going to use it, so I'm not taking it home with me!" Mae finally relented, and the morphine was placed back on the shelf.

But then, the coup de grâce. She told me that we could not leave without signing a POLST (Physician's Orders for Life-Sustaining Treatment), a non-resuscitation order, which would legally prevent first responders from giving Nissi any medical treatment! In total shock, I adamantly refused to sign such a thing. Mae, thoroughly frustrated with my stubbornness, finally told me that Dr. Ralph would call me in our room.

A few minutes later, the phone rang. It was Dr. Ralph. "Elie, you need to sign the POLST," he instructed.

I refused point-blank. "Ralph, you know that this is against my religion," I said, letting the word "my" hang in the air.

Ralph wouldn't be swayed. "What if the police stop you on your way home and see the baby blue in the back of the car?" he asked. The question itself was nonsensical; we lived a scant ten city blocks away from the hospital. What would I get pulled over for?! But in any case, I was utterly dumbfounded that he could say such a thing.

"What do you mean?! I'll tell him that *you* refused to give him medical care!"

"But what will you do when they ask you for the POLST?"

I rejoined, "I'll tell him that it's against my religion to sign something like that!"

Eventually, sounding resigned, he agreed to allow us to leave, but informed the staff that we had to take a printed POLST form, even if we did not sign it. Mae handed me the bright-green paper. I didn't even look at it, and just dropped it into the massive stack of medical papers and hospital informational brochures.

In a move that truly depicted the insanity of everything going on, the social worker appeared. Remembering my aversion toward contacting the *chevrah kaddisha*, the Jewish Burial Society, before the baby's birth, she handed Chaya a flowery "Thinking of You" card. "I've written the contact information for the *chevrah kaddisha* in this card. We thought this way it might be easier for your husband to handle," she said to my wife, giggling. The card joined the POLST in the pile of discharge papers.

WE WERE ALL PACKED UP and had somewhere to go—but quickly. However, we had one more dilemma to overcome—we didn't have a car seat with us. When coming to the hospital for the birth, we hadn't brought one with us. After all, if he was going into surgery, he wouldn't need one. And he wouldn't need a car seat for the other possibility either...Knowing that hospitals have car seats for new mothers who can't afford them, I asked Mae if we could borrow one. "I live a few blocks away, so I can bring it right back," I told her.

"Oh, you don't need one," she responded breezily. "We'll write you a note. You can carry him home on your lap." Shocked, but anxious to leave the hospital that had become nothing but a morgue-in-waiting, we did so, despite Dr. Ralph's request to wait until he arrived. I very slowly drove home; Chaya held him carefully, seated in the back seat of our old Ford Explorer.

Getting home was a massive relief, but our nerves were as taut as could be. The very first thing I did as soon as I entered my house was dig out that "death" card from the social worker. Handling it like it was contaminated, I proceeded to deposit it directly into the trash can. I distinctly remember wishing that I had a bonfire to throw it into.

Soon after we arrived home, a hospice nurse arrived to have us sign documents to enroll us in their system. We again refused the hospice nurse visitations, making it clear that we were only signing into the program because our arms had been twisted. She finally began to take us seriously once I explained that I'd been trained as a Seattle Police and US Air Force chaplain, and our attitude was not the result of grief or cluelessness, but of a deliberate methodology. She quickly handed us the papers to sign and left.

As she walked out of the house, an older man, whom I'd never seen before, entered. In a sarcastic mood, I welcomed him in with a quip. "Oh my gosh, it's Doc Brown!" I called out, referencing his wild white hair to that of the mad scientist in the *Back to the Future* movies. Surprised, he introduced himself as a photographer for a volunteer organization called Now I Lay Me Down to Sleep. In truly macabre fashion, they take pictures of babies who have left this world or are on their way out as a keepsake for the parents. We had been offered their "services" at each OB visit by the social worker assigned to our case these past nine weeks. We'd refused it strenuously every time. But apparently, while I'd been busy arguing with Mae just before we'd left the hospital, Chaya had agreed to them coming. "We're alive and so is the baby, so if you want to send a photographer to take pictures of us, be my guest," she shrugged. So here he was.

He had walked in as I was finishing my morning prayers, while I was busy removing my tefillin, with my tallis still draped over my shoulders. I explained my getup to the surprised photographer. "Pardon me, this is the Jewish security blanket," I remarked jokingly in reference to my tallis, delirious sarcasm still exhibiting itself in my speech. "This is how we Jews pray." A thought flickered across my addled mind. "Do you happen to be Jewish?" I asked, with no expectation of a positive response.

"In fact, I am," he responded.

My heart leaped, and I jumped at the opportunity. "Would you like to put on tefillin?" I asked.

"If you'd allow a secular Jew to do so, I'd be honored," he said.

A wave of joy engulfed me. "It would be the greatest pleasure if you did!" And I brought him over to the dining room table, where he put on tefillin for the first time in many decades since his son's bar mitzvah.

Dr. Ralph had refused my offer to help him don tefillin a few times, telling me that while he'd love to, he didn't think it was appropriate to do a mitzvah not for G-d's sake but for a human's sake. I'd argued against that false sense of holiness, but he was unmovable. Now, the tension we were under dissipated in the glow of true holiness. The house brightened up visibly with the photographer's mitzvah. I felt that perhaps this was the reason we had undergone all we had, just so this one Jew would put on tefillin...Perhaps this was the fulfillment of our precious baby boy's mission...Joyously, we recited *Shema* together, and the photographer asked for pictures that he could send to his own son. He followed our tefillin session with taking several black-and-white shots of us holding Nissi, one of which adorns the cover of this book.

The children came home from school soon afterward, and with them came all the excitement of having a new baby in the house. Yet Chaya and I were quite jumpy, watching the baby like hawks, and massaging his entire body every time he tinged purple. Chaya barely let him out of her hands. At this point, only my two oldest children knew that Nissi was deathly ill; the younger three only knew vaguely that he was sick.

Finally back in our own home, as we tried to recover some semblance of sanity, I remembered one clear thought—this experience was diametrically against everything Judaism stands for. Over the years, we had taught a course to college students about the relevance of the Ten Commandments to contemporary society. I had always enjoyed teaching the class on "Do Not Murder," passionately explaining that murder is defined by Judaism as the forced separation of body and soul, explaining how abortion and assisted suicide often fall into that category. And here we were, our own son being cornered by those whose job was ostensibly to heal, but were instead almost gleefully awaiting his funeral. It was truly horrific. We felt as though our hands had been shackled, and we'd been powerless to do anything about it.

Yet Nissi had survived until this point, so we hoped for some more time—and then maybe a medical team could be found that would take on his case.

THE ALMOST UNBEARABLE TENSION and lack of sleep left us utterly exhausted and unable to think clearly. Somewhere in the recesses of my dysfunctional mind, I knew that we needed to do something, but I was simply physically and emotionally unable to make any phone calls or do any internet research to that end. Everything was too overwhelming during those hazy hours. Instead, I opted for sleep. "If he survives the night, I'll call East Coast doctors first thing in the morning," I brainlessly informed Chaya.

The Book of Esther uses a climactic description of the events that led to the ultimate turnaround: "On that night, the King's sleep was disturbed."[5] And we, in our little world, experienced our own version of that epic verse toward the end of yet another night of restlessness.

At five o'clock in the morning, the baby's sleep was disturbed, directly on time for his every two-hour feed schedule. Crying and fussing, he demanded to be fed. A voice spoke to me through the haze of my sleep—Chaya asked me to prepare a bottle of formula. I stumbled out of bed, and in my zombie-like state, neglected to put the top of the bottle on tight, and the formula spilled all over the bed.

Only rare women are as calm as Chaya is on a regular day, but after the hellish week, her utter exhaustion peaked. In her delirium, she lashed out at me. "You didn't put the top on! You made me spill!" I immediately apologized. "I'm so sorry!" I stuttered sleepily, as I found a towel and tried to wipe up the spilled milk in the darkness. Her response was comical, considering the truly considerate and fine woman she is. "You should be!" she cried out. I tried to apologize once again. She was having none of it, and repeated herself, "You should be!"

After cleaning things up as well I could, I crawled back under the covers. But having been roundly chastised by my sleepy wife, I was now wide awake, sans caffeine. "Why in the world am I getting back into bed? Enough is enough! It's time to call doctors on the East Coast." With that thought, I jumped out of bed and ran upstairs to my office. Both emotion and exhaustion were pushed aside as I got to work.

When Chaya was still pregnant, several people had provided me with names and numbers of supposed miracle-working surgeons. I had not seriously considered contacting them before, as we'd been continuously told—nay, in*doctri*nated—that his ultra-unique anatomy left no medical options whatsoever. Now was the time to make use of those names and numbers. After several calls and e-mails, a medical referral coordinator, Rabbi Avraham Lieder, put me in touch with an observant Jewish pediatric cardiologist in New York, Dr. Rubin Cooper.

Dr. Cooper heard me out and calmly replied, "You probably know that Washington State was the first state to allow euthanasia. I believe

---

5   *Esther* 6:1.

that you've been a victim of the 'Death with Dignity' movement. If the baby is alive, there is definitely something that can be done for him. Your doctors were wrong medically, ethically, and halachically. You absolutely can and **must** find someone to operate on him!" New hope was born. I felt a tremendous weight fall off my shoulders, and I profusely thanked Dr. Cooper.

Freshly invigorated, an idea popped into my head. I thought maybe Dr. Fern could give us some direction on how to keep the baby alive until we'd find a hospital that would be willing to operate; at the very least, maybe Seattle Children's would be willing to keep him in their ICU until we found such a surgeon and could transport him wherever we needed to go. With that in mind, at 7:00 a.m., I called the Seattle Children's Hospital cardiac emergency line, and described the situation, asking for Dr. Fern to call us back.

Dr. Fern returned my call at exactly 9:00 a.m., remarking in surprise, "But we had been told that you refused the surgical option!"

I rejoined, "I told you clearly from the outset we were going to do everything we could for the baby. We were told that due to his complexity, Children's refused his case, and I understand that, but..."

Dr. Fern interrupted me. "Seattle Children's Hospital would never turn down a child. How quickly can you get here?"

I was stunned. "Uh, maybe five minutes?!" I replied. We lived just a short mile and a half away.

"All right," she said. "I'm going to make a cardiology appointment for you for ten o'clock. You'll need to pack up some clothes and supplies for overnight; the baby will be in surgery tonight."

The sudden rush of joy that hit me was indescribable. To quote the Book of Esther once again, "And everything was turned around."[6] The agony and fear that had hung over us for nine weeks simply disappeared.

The moment that I hung up with Dr. Fern, a haggard-looking Chaya stumbled downstairs for breakfast and coffee. I practically sang

---

6   *Esther* 9:1.

out, "Chaya, pack up for Shabbos—the baby's going to surgery tonight! We have forty-five minutes to get to Children's Hospital!"

"What?" she looked at me in complete surprise.

"I'll explain in the car!" I called back. Unhesitatingly, she turned around and ran back upstairs, while my parents-in-law and I quickly made Shabbos plans and spread responsibilities around: deciding where the children would go, who would arrange Shabbos meals, and, with the newfound joy, asking someone to make a *shalom zachar*, the traditional "welcoming the baby" Shabbos celebration for us. The tiny spark of positivity and hope now roared into a full-fledged bonfire. And so, the next chapter began.

Chapter 3

Welcome to Children's Hospital

W e virtually skipped into Dr. Matt Files's cardiology office at Seattle Children's Hospital. I launched into an admittedly corny mood, with the inner hope that with our humor and positivity, we'd win over the entire staff, and fresh and honest effort would be exerted to save Nissi's life.

Dr. Files would later comment how he noted that when we arrived at his office, Nissi's skin tone virtually matched Chaya's blueish-purple shirt. In fact, we wouldn't really "meet" Nissi's true skin color for several months, as he changed daily from a pale, wan white to purple and occasionally gray and back again, depending on his body's reactions to procedures, oxygen saturation rates, or whatever else was going on. We later joked that we should have had a time-lapse camera on him to record his chameleon-like appearance!

Internally, I was struck by my own change of perspective. In early January, I had brought our toddler Menachi to Children's for a checkup on his sinuses, which seemed to be perpetually stuffed up. At the time, I walked into the building and fairly spat at the thought of being trapped there with our, as of yet unborn, baby. And now, the joy at being admitted into the very same institution filled every fiber of my being! Now I had a new, personal perspective on the idea of referring to a hospital as a "Place of Healing."

An extended echocardiogram confirmed the cardiac diagnosis, but the team rejected the existence of esophageal atresia by giving him a quick swallow study, feeding him a dye, and watching it go down his GI system on an ultrasound. (Wasn't this the type of testing we wanted as soon as he was born?!) That study seemed to show that he had a hiatal hernia, which the doctors predicted would give Nissi trouble with reflux in the future. They were quite surprised that he'd been bottle feeding so well; in fact, he had not spit up at all during those first days of his life. After an hour of testing, Dr. Files returned. He reviewed the results, confirming that Nissi was indeed a candidate for open heart surgery. We felt the burden of responsibility begin to lift as the nurses wheeled Nissi to the Cardiac ICU(CICU).

In the CICU, Nissi's first nurse introduced herself as Vivian, which immediately called to mind Chaya's own Aunt Viv. As she began to hook up Nissi to an IV, I giddily remarked, "You have never seen parents so thrilled to be in the ICU in your entire career!" Things began to settle down.

Suddenly, one of the doctors pointed out that his oxygen saturation numbers were tanking. "You see," he said to Chaya, "that's his patent ductus arteriosus closing up. You got here in the nick of time!" With a fresh dose of prostaglandin doing its magic, his oxygen sats stabilized.

Late that afternoon, my phone rang. It was the hospice nurse calling to check on things in her usual mournful tone. "I just wanted to check in on you," she carefully asked, expecting somber news to follow. "How are you doing?"

"Things are great!" I sang out. "We're going into surgery tonight, so we won't need your services."

"Wha—" came a stuttering voice on the other end. After a few moments of disjointed stammering, the hospice nurse finally pulled herself together and said, "In that case, we'll have to separate you from our system! Insurance won't pay for the operation if the baby is still registered in hospice."

"Please do! I never wanted him to be in hospice in the first place!" I said, with sweet vindication filling the line.

In the meantime, I received an e-mail from Dr. Ralph, who noted that he had "heard the good news" (possibly via our posts on Facebook) and wanted to know if he could stop by to say hello on Shabbos. At this point, we obviously wanted nothing to do with him, and I told him so in an e-mail. The closest thing to an apology that we'd receive from him would be an e-mail that read, "I'm sorry for the breakdown in communication," which only served to infuriate us more. We instructed the charge nurse to make sure that he would not have permission to come to our bedside, to which she willingly and forcefully agreed. She seemed to be as upset as we were about all that had transpired.

Shabbos was coming quickly. The staff knew and understood our restrictions and worked expeditiously to get things settled for us. Dr. Rubio, the cardiologist responsible for catheterizations, came by to go over the details of the surgery and get signed permission for the upcoming procedure before Shabbos began. He explained the complicated operation clearly and intelligently.

Dr. Jeffries, one of the ICU intensivists, came over as well to give us the schedule for the evening. He concluded with a cryptic look and said, "One more thing—have a wonderful Shabbos!" That brought a huge smile to my face, and I said, "You're Jewish? Would you like to join us for Shabbos dinner tonight in the parents' lounge?" He laughed and pointed to a young woman just outside our room. "I'm going home for Shabbos dinner with my family, but Emily here is also a member of the tribe. Maybe she'd like to join you!" A surprised Dr. Emily, an ICU fellow with classic Jewish features, was then introduced to us. Hers was a friendly face we'd become very familiar with.

A little later, our surgeon savior came by to introduce himself. He was Dr. David McMullan, and we could tell from our brief conversation that he and we were on the same page. Somehow, we fell into a discussion about medical ethics, and when I told him Judaism's approach, that of focusing on life itself over the relativistic quality of life, he concurred. "I agree with that. I try to save any baby who comes in here, no matter the odds." The relief that we finally had a medical staff that would actually do their job was just beyond description. We felt like we'd finally found the allies we had been struggling so hard to find. The irony that they had been waiting for us (a mere mile away from our home!) was beyond comprehension.

Dr. McMullan was deeply touched by the concept that the soul has a purpose in every moment that it is in a body, and later asked if we could help him find someone to present Judaism's view of medical ethics for a conference on the subject that he was organizing. We happily agreed to do so and put him in touch with a local rabbi who is a renowned ethicist.

THE OUTSIDE WORLD had known precious few of the details of our struggles. But by now, the word had gotten out that we had a baby who was deathly ill. We sent out a birth notice via Facebook and e-mail on Thursday, with a request for people to recite *Tehillim* and perform mitzvos in his merit. Thankfully, this e-mail was nothing like the one I had conjured in my mind dozens of times over the previous three months. The news of his impending open-heart surgery spread like wildfire across the world, throughout our extended network of family, friends, and colleagues. We felt a deluge of spiritual and communal support as we headed into Shabbos.

A *shalom zachar* was quickly arranged to be held at a friend's house. Not surprisingly, I was too exhausted to walk there and join in person. But my father-in-law took my place instead, and toasts were made over words of Torah and joyful singing in the baby's honor.

We celebrated Shabbos with a meal provided by friends in the community, sitting at a table for two in the parents' lounge. Dr. Emily came by to say hello, and I again invited her to join us. I laughed at our situation and pointed out that Shabbos has been celebrated in stranger places, such as during the Holocaust, because Shabbos remains eternal no matter the circumstances. She was visibly touched, but she was on call and could not stay long.

Our next Shabbos guest was Dr. McMullan, who walked in directly from a surgical conference deliberating Nissi's case. He sat down and accepted our invitation to join our little meal. We began discussing two surgical options over a piece of delicious cinnamon challah. One option was to do a complete surgery, which would include inserting a Blalock-Taussig shunt in place of the pulmonary valve (creating a pathway for blood between the heart and lungs), as well as repairing the pulmonary veins and now open PDA, while the other option was to do a temporary catheterization procedure until things were stabilized.

We discussed the different possibilities, and at some point in the conversation, got down to asking about the success rates of the various procedures. But Dr. McMullan turned to us with a pointed look and a little smile. "Look, if you'd have told me about a kid with Nissi's degree of heart disease going home for four days with no medical intervention, I'd give him a zero percent chance of survival. And here's your son—right now he's the most stable kid in the unit!" He was absolutely confident that whatever choice we'd make, Nissi would do well.

In the end, we decided on the full surgery. After all, it was necessary no matter what, and a catheterization would be just a delay of the inevitable. Chaya asked him when they were planning on doing the surgery, considering the lateness of the hour, and he responded, "Whenever you want. The team is here, and we're ready to go, but if you want to do it tomorrow first thing, he'll be fine overnight."

Chaya laughingly said, "I think I'd like you and the team to get some sleep before you operate on my son's heart!" He laughed, and as he rose, he agreed with that plan. "Pre-op will be at eight o'clock in the morning. I'll see you then!"

Another long night was in store for us, but we were emotionally in a different universe than we'd been in the previous nights. Nissi needed a lot of comforting; however, no longer were we in the mental space of desperation or dread. We were finally absent of that abject fear that we'd wake up holding a body bereft of its soul. Instead, we now felt full of the hope and tranquility of confidence and trust—"Nissi, you'll be okay." We had the emotional stamina to comfort and care for our sick little boy. Chaya took the longest shift holding him, and I slept uncomfortably on a recliner that wouldn't recline.

The morning light eventually broke through the window of the room, and we awoke to see a refreshed Dr. McMullan, a cup of coffee in his hand. The team took Nissi for his pre-op tests, and just before he left the room, I leaned over and recited an emotion-filled *birkas habanim*, the special blessing a father gives his children, which in my community is usually given during the magical, spiritual moments before the onset of Yom Kippur. I also asked Dr. McMullan to stop the team during their pre-op huddle, and, in our name, ask everyone to take on a personal positive resolution in the merit of the baby. He smiled and firmly agreed to do so.

During surgery, we felt embraced and buoyed by the worldwide spiritual support we had received over the past few days. A nurse came in occasionally to give updates. "He's on the heart/lung machine!" "He's off the heart/lung machine!" And yet there we were, calmly or even joyfully praying and saying *Tehillim*! I remarked as much to Chaya, and we both agreed that our feelings of absolute calm were the result of both the worldwide support we had and the miraculous journey that we'd thus far traveled. After all, Jewish thought teaches that G-d doesn't do miracles for naught.[1]

In between chapters of *Tehillim*, we got to talking with our nurse about the surgery. "Have you ever been inside the operating room during one of these surgeries?" Chaya asked. The nurse nodded energetically. "Absolutely! It's an incredible thing to see." She held out her fist to us. "An adult's heart is approximately the size of your fist, so think about how small your baby's heart is. The baby's veins are tiny; almost as small as fishing line! The surgeon wears glasses with a device like a microscope on it in order to see what he's doing. And as he works, he's dealing with such minuscule repairs that it looks like his hands aren't even moving!" We were awed, and still are, by that description.

After five hours in surgery, we were informed that the surgeons were sewing Nissi back up. Dr. Geiduschek, the anesthesiologist, came out of the operating room first, and with a large smile on his face, said, "He did really well!" Dr. McMullan came out later. He reported, "We even managed to close his chest—that's the surgical equivalent of hitting a homerun!"

Dr. McMullan had informed us beforehand that the trickiest part of the surgery was the pulmonary vein repair, owing to the small size of the veins and the intensity of the blood pressure at the spot where the veins would need to be connected to the heart. In response to our

---

1   See *Drashos HaRa"n, Drush* 8 (Jerusalem: Katzenelenbogen, 2003 edition), p. 298.

question about how that part of the surgery went, he enthusiastically responded, "I think that was the best vein repair I've ever done!"

He was equally optimistic about Nissi's recuperation but reminded us that he'd probably have a honeymoon period followed by several difficult days. Sure enough, toward the end of Shabbos, things started to go crazy.

The nurse that evening moved like a rabbit, bouncing from the IV to the computer and back again, constantly readjusting all the medications. Nissi was hooked up to a forest of IVs, with tubes and wires protruding from what seemed like every inch of his little body. His lactate level—a measurement of acid in the blood, coming from infection or circulatory shock—soared, reaching a peak of seventeen. (Normal is below one, and they stop measuring lactate after twenty.)

Things started to get really intense toward the end of Shabbos as his instability peaked, and nurses and doctors swarmed his bed. A cardiac fellow I had nicknamed "The Jolly Good Fellow," Dr. Jesse, pulled out the defibrillator at some point to administer a shock, but thankfully he didn't need it, as Nissi stabilized somewhat. But seeing the chaos and not wanting to get in the way, we headed for the Quiet Room at the end of the ICU.

Noticing us, Dr. McMullan sympathetically followed us into the room. He encouraged us, saying, "Don't worry about everything in there; he'll pull through. And the medical fellows need some excitement. It's good for them!" We appreciated his good-natured laughter. Utterly exhausted, we fell asleep on the couches in the Quiet Room until after Shabbos. By that time, everything had settled down somewhat, but Nissi was obviously still extremely ill.

Over the next few days, they still struggled to lower his lactate, and an irregular heart rhythm that we nicknamed "the salsa" occasionally appeared. His heart rate would shoot up like a rocket, from regular numbers in the low one hundreds to dangerous numbers in the mid-two hundreds, which was a very unhealthy place to be.

That lactate was a major issue. The nurses took blood samples every two hours to check the latest levels, and on the occasion that the number dropped, we'd let out a mighty cheer. But in those early days, when it spiked and refused to come down after two days, Dr. Titus, a young cardiologist and the spiffiest dresser in the unit, told me that he'd like us to have a conversation with the palliative care team. I was having none of it.

"Is he doing that badly yet?" I queried.

"No," he admitted, "but if we can't get him to drop his lactate, he'll need to go on ECMO [extracorporeal membrane oxygenation—a life-saving yet life-threatening contraption that cleans and recirculates the blood for the heart], and when that happens, we have a policy that the family needs to speak to palliative care."

I interrupted him quickly. "Listen, your job is to work on him right now, and not to worry about the what-ifs. Our job is to focus on the positive. We've had enough of palliative care at our previous hospital, and it's not going to be of any help to the baby. So instead of worrying about us, get back in there and figure him out!"

Titus didn't seem to be too ruffled by my speech, so I concluded it by harping on how a doctor should provide parents and patients with a little bit of positive grip tape to hold them up, as opposed to constantly focusing on the negative. He finally relented, saying, "But if things get worse, I'm going to insist that you speak with palliative care." To that I reluctantly agreed, eager to get him off my back, and he headed back into the room to consult with the nurses.

Later, I told the nurses that our new catchphrase was "Say No to ECMO!" That got a good laugh and reinjected lightheartedness into the room.

IN ORDER TO CONTINUE all the good spiritual vibes, as well as to keep concerned friends and family informed, I began daily Facebook and WhatsApp posts. I had no idea to what extent people would take to them. Dozens of groups sprang up all over, whose members split up the entire book of *Tehillim* for some unknown little baby across the globe. Messages of love and support kept pouring in with every post. Nissi garnered a fan base that was quite extensive.

Even now, several years later, every "Nissi Update" social media post pulls in reactions from people we've never met. Every so often, I'm asked, "Are you Nissi's father?" Or, alternatively, "We've been following your story since the beginning." Most people also had no idea that we tailored those posts with a positive vibe in order to maintain the "think good" angle, both for ourselves and others. Only medical personnel were able to see through the cheer and realize how dicey things got at particular points in the journey.

AS THE DAYS PROGRESSED, we found ourselves in a basic routine of getting the kids to school (oftentimes, they were driven by our parents or other sanity savers) and then getting to the hospital in time for rounds. During those first weeks, my parents-in-law were keeping watch on the older children. Later, my own parents came for a few weeks as well.

Sometimes, Chaya and I would head out for lunch; otherwise, we'd hang out in Nissi's room while the kids were in school, talking between ourselves and with the medical team, stroking Nissi's head or arm, and saying *Tehillim*. About twice a week, the children would come to the hospital to visit Nissi, splitting their time between the CICU and the hospital playroom. A few times, we even took them swimming in the hospital therapy pool. Homework went totally out the window; schoolwork simply took a backseat to sanity.

At the end of every evening at home, if we had the energy and a babysitter, we'd grab another few hours in the hospital. Evenings always ended with a quick call to the CICU for an update on our fighter, and as soon as we woke up the next morning, another such call. What a relief it was on the occasions that the nurses had nothing to report.

Rounds featured prominently in our daily routine. In the CICU, staff conversation is run extremely efficiently, with representatives of all medical disciplines listening in and adding whatever information was deemed crucial. They'd begin with his nurse, followed by the nutritionist, pharmacist, and then the cardiologist, culminating with the plan of the day developed by the medical fellow, with interjections by the ICU intensivist.

Chaya and I would ask questions in order to understand things better, and occasionally (okay, maybe more than occasionally) toss in jokes, lightening things up. One of the more humorous moments was when once, as the doctors went through Nissi's massive medication list,

Chaya tossed in, "Oh, did we forget to tell you that we're anti-vaxxers?" The entire staff besides the pharmacist knew that Chaya had been kidding, so all collapsed into laughter. When brought into the joke, the poor pharmacist exhaled deeply in obvious relief.

During rounds on one of the early days, as Nissi's medical history was being reviewed, I heard the doctor say, "The baby was placed in non-invasive palliative care, but then the parents changed their minds and brought him to surgery." I was furious and angrily insisted that they change the notes to reflect the reality of what had occurred—that we had been given incorrect information that his condition was inoperable. Thankfully, the medical notes attached to his record were duly corrected.

Truth be told, whenever a new member of Nissi's medical staff heard of his first few days of life, they would stand openmouthed, utterly appalled. One nurse told us she was ashamed for her profession. We later heard that one of the nurses at University Hospital actually quit because of how we were treated. She told a friend that she refused to work for an institution in which such a thing could happen.

We made a choice early on in our journey not to sleep at the hospital, knowing that we'd need to maintain our own sanity as well as keep life as stable and predictable for the other children. As mentioned, before going to sleep and immediately when waking up, we'd call the hospital to find out what was going on. On rare occasions, they'd call us. Due to the urgency of his condition, our phones were on and accessible on Shabbos, a time when observant Jews do not use electric devices, and so when the phone rang one Shabbos afternoon, my heart leaped into my throat. I hesitated to pick up, though, as I knew Nissi was stable at that point, and let the call drop. Yet whoever was on the other end redialed immediately. Could something have gone wrong? Knowing that the usual rule precluding usage of electricity on Shabbos takes a back seat to emergencies, I answered the phone with trepidation. "Hello?"

The voice on the other line was anything but urgent. "Hi! This is so-and-so from lactation services…"

She didn't get any further, as I cut her off with a curt, "Can't talk now," and hung up the phone. My heart rate stayed at salsa levels for another hour or two.

Before the next Shabbos, we told the medical staff not to call us until after seven o'clock on Saturday night unless it was an emergency. In reality, Shabbos was over at 7:02; but who thought specifying the time down to the minute was necessary? Well, at precisely 7:00 p.m., the phone rang, and caller ID revealed it was from Children's. The next two minutes felt like a year! But it ended up being just hematology calling with a routine question. Ugh.

THE FEAR INDUCED by a call from the ICU was not due to mere frazzled worry and unconnected to reality. On February 16, at about 4:00 a.m., just a few days after surgery, my phone rang. I answered groggily. Dr. Banker, one of the ICU intensivists, was on the line. Nissi's lactate was not getting any better, and they decided to reopen his chest to allow the swelling more room in order to alleviate the pressure on the heart. "Do whatever you need to do," I told her.

Surgery number two went well, and over the next few days, things started to calm down, until medication by medication, tube by tube, machines and IV drips were removed. By February 22, things had improved to the point that they could close his chest once again, and thankfully, surgery number three was deemed a success.

But despite arranging emergency communication, every Shabbos was nerve-racking. Thankfully, we knew a pair of angels who lived right across the street from Seattle Children's Hospital. Uri and Avigayil London would visit Nissi several times over Shabbos to sing Shabbos songs, hold him, and provide him with an atmosphere of Shabbos in the sterile CICU ward. They were truly heaven sent, allowing us to relax with our other children, let go of some of the tension (as much as that was possible), and enjoy Shabbos. On occasion, I'd walk over to the hospital on Shabbos afternoon to see what was going on, sometimes prompted by a nagging, unfounded worry that would pop up in my own or Chaya's mind, which would annoyingly refuse to go away and only intensify over the hours. Typically, my walk would turn into a brisk jog as I got closer, as disaster scenarios played out in my head, propelled by a hyperactive imagination. Breathless and somewhat fearful, I'd enter his room, and the nurse would greet me with, "He's doing great!" At that point I'd collapse on the couch in relief. When I didn't make the mile-and-a-half trek, we'd ring in for an update immediately after Shabbos was over.

On February 19, Nissi was welcomed back to the world of feeding. The nutritionist, a lovely Argentinian woman named Claudia, took it upon herself to get her "bambino" to put on some weight. With her formula concoctions, he finally started to gain some weight, and soon his nurses were joking about his "Claudia cheeks."

Those were some of the good days. From February 23 to February 27, several lines and tubes were removed, including a successful extubation from the breathing tube. On February 26, Chaya was finally able to snuggle with her baby for the first time since she had handed him to the doctors for his first surgery, or at least as much as the remaining lines and tubes allowed.

During those days, we had a few personal encounters that were particularly moving. Dr. Baden, the head of the ICU, came by during rounds. With a very pleasant expression, he asked us about our children, and we told him we had five in addition to Nissi. "What are their names?" he queried.

"Our eldest is Yehuda, and he's eleven."

"Yehuda," he mused, pronouncing the name perfectly. "And the next?"

"Shayna is nine," I said.

"Shayna! As in *shayna punim* [sweet face]!" he said with a broad smile, proud of his Yiddishism.

"All right, now you blew your cover!" I cried out joyously. And, indeed, Dr. Baden was a proud Jew, and we had some wonderful conversations with him.

But an exchange with Dr. Emily blew all our minds. With the enactment of a typical game of Jewish Geography, she revealed that her parents were from "a small suburb of Cleveland."

"Oh! My parents are from Cleveland; where are your parents from?"

"South Euclid."

Stunned, I responded, "That's where my father grew up!"

It turns out that her parents went to the same high school as my father, probably at about the same time as my father's sister, and her grandmother lived in the same apartment complex as my grandmother.

But the bigger deal was when she texted her grandmother with my grandparents' names…and her grandmother remembered some of my relatives from high school! Talk about landsleit, fellow countrymen, and an incredible memory to boot!

A FEW WEEKS INTO THE JOURNEY, we thought it was about time to explain to the kids what was going on with their brother. Seattle Children's had a special family social worker. She arranged to have a surgical fellow who'd been involved with Nissi's surgeries to talk with us and answer any questions the kids might have. Dr. Farraz Shaw was a tall Indian gentleman, and he brought detailed drawings of Nissi's heart that he'd traced with an authentic fountain pen. As he tried explaining Nissi's complex anatomy to the group of confused children, Chaya and I finally began understanding things ourselves. The poor kids couldn't understand a thing, however.

Only Naomi had a question. "What does his heart feel like?" she wondered.

Dr. Shaw smiled and pointed to the palm of his hand. "Like this," he said, stroking the skin below his thumb.

I asked Dr. Shaw what he thought about Nissi surviving the first five days. "Was it because his PDA, that hole between the heart and lungs, miraculously stayed open that long?" I asked, perhaps pushing the miracle narrative a bit.

"Well," he answered slowly, "the PDA staying open was indeed a big deal, but that wasn't really the biggest deal."

"What do you mean?" I queried.

Dr. Shaw looked perplexed as he responded. "The PDA is just an absolutely tiny hole. It allows a very small amount of blood flow through. We really have no idea how he had such high oxygen saturations for those first few days, even *with* the PDA staying open!"

This admission of wonder coming from someone who explored Nissi's cardiac anatomy with his own hands…

AT ABOUT THIS TIME, I started getting nervous about what to do about a bris. When should the ritual circumcision take place, if ever?

A local mohel, Rabbi Schtroks, relieved my fears when he explained that doing a bris on an unhealthy child would not fulfill the religious requirement appropriately. Still, he told me to call a halachic expert in Australia, Rabbi Faitel Levin, for a clear directive on what to do. Rabbi Levin instructed us to have the baby-naming prayer, typically recited at the *bris milah*, said for him at the very next Torah reading, thereby making his name "official" from the Jewish perspective, but not to worry about the circumcision itself until after the next corrective surgery, which we knew would not take place for quite some time.

We were thrilled to follow his instructions. While we'd been calling him Nesanel/Nissi this entire time, we were excited to make it official. In addition, we felt that naming him in the presence of the Torah scroll would give him additional spiritual power and permanence represented by the holiness of the Torah itself.

The feelings that prompted the name choice in the first place, that his life was a gift from G-d, remained strong on a day-by-day basis, and it still rings loud and clear today—a single name with a singular message. The very next morning, I went to the synagogue and officially named him at the Torah. The message flashed out to all our social media groups. He was no longer the semi-anonymous Tinok *ben* Chaya Rochel ("Baby, son of Chaya Rochel"); he was now officially Nesanel *ben* Chaya Rochel.

WITH ALL THE GOOD VIBES coming from medication weans, growth, and feeds (even by mouth), he graduated to the post-surgical floor on Friday, March 4. He threw an absolute fit as he left the CICU, but was soon quieted down as we got him settled in his new room with his new nurses.

Despite all the assurances that this move meant he was much more stable and home was on the horizon, both Chaya and I felt very ill at ease, although we couldn't quite put our finger on why.

Chapter 4

Another Call in the Night

O ver Shabbos, tragedy struck close to home. We found out
on Saturday night that good friends of ours lost their
four-month-old baby to SIDS. The news hit us hard. When
we visited Nissi on Sunday evening, I still found myself conflicted and
consumed with survivors' guilt. Here, our son who wasn't supposed
to survive was looking up at me with his sweet little eyes, while our
friends' arms were empty. Nissi, however, was calm, and spending time
with him was therapeutic. He happily consumed eighteen milliliters of
milk by mouth using the binky trainer system, and when we left that
night, we were a little more relaxed. The nurse, Carly, assured us that
she'd do her best to take care of him, as she had the previous two nights.
She was a chatty and caring young nurse and did her best to alleviate
any concerns we had before we left.

That night, while we slept, a silent killer lurked unchecked.

LIFE ON THE POST-SURGICAL FLOOR is very different than
in the CICU. While day and night seem interchangeable in the CICU,
nighttime on the floor is pretty dull. The hallways are quiet, the children are sleeping, the nurses seem to disappear for long stretches of
time as they monitor their patients remotely, and the residents, fresh
out of medical school, are officially in charge and learning on the job.
The senior doctors are primarily on call from off-site.

At about 2:30 a.m., Carly was ready for her "lunch" break. As per the
usual system, she asked a fellow nurse, a close friend of hers, to keep
watch on all four of her charges while she went to the lunchroom to eat.

Now the new nurse was responsible for eight children—in the middle of the night—with almost no one around to help out.

Nissi was not yet eating enough to sustain himself, so he was being fed via a pump that was giving him feeds around the clock. The pump's milk bag, which holds about four hours' worth of milk, was almost empty. Carly had planned to refill the bag before leaving on break, but she forgot.

Five minutes later, with Carly on break, the milk ran out, and the pump alarm began to ring. The substitute nurse came into Nissi's room to silence the alarm and refill the bag of milk. As she did so, she glanced at the sleeping baby and noticed that he'd slipped partially under his blanket. She removed the blanket from his face but was immediately alarmed by the color of his skin tone—gray. She called Carly on her phone, with concern evident in her voice. "Does he always look this gray?" Carly, hearing the urgency, recognized that something was very wrong and literally dropped her meal and sprinted across the hospital to get back to Nissi's bedside.

As Carly arrived breathlessly, she likewise noted his ashen color and heavy work of breathing. Quickly assessing the situation, she told her friend to call the rapid response team—ICU doctors—to take a look at him. As her friend picked up the phone to do so, Carly saw Nissi's heart rate and oxygen saturations, which had been holding steady, suddenly begin to drop, and she cried out, "Code Blue!"

Immediately, the other nurse hit the emergency button on the wall. "Code Blue, 4th floor, room 422, bedspace 2," rang out over the hospital loudspeakers, echoing in the empty hallways.

Within seconds, Room 422 filled with people. Nissi's eleven-year-old roommate was immediately whisked off to another room, with his terrified father glancing over his shoulder like Lot's wife at the scene behind them. Bright lights flooded the room, and medical professionals of every discipline rushed in to provide assistance. Alarms pealed and were ignored. Nissi's heart rate and oxygen level continued to drop precipitously. A woman jumped on his bed and began CPR. Incredibly, she was a respiratory therapist—the very most skilled person in the hospital to administer CPR!—and had been in the room directly next door. With incredible focus and speed, Nissi was intu-bated once again. Life-saving medication was administered through his IV and PICC line. This itself was a small miracle, as the plan had been to remove the PICC line the very next day. But since it was still there, they were able to give a large variety of drugs directly into his bloodstream via both lines.

As they wheeled him out of his room, a medical fellow sat in the crib doing chest compressions, and they sped him across the hospital back to the CICU. The team worked feverishly to get back inside the heart, discover the culprit that caused the cardiac arrest, and solve the problem. In order to keep his body alive, the decision was quickly made to get him hooked up to the ECMO pump—a machine that does all the work of the heart and lungs while allowing them to stabilize and hopefully heal. Within just fifty minutes of the arrest—all fifty of those precious minutes spent doing continuous CPR to keep his heart functioning steadily despite its precarious state—his chest was already reopened and he was successfully hooked up to the ECMO pump. We were later told that it couldn't have happened any faster, even if he had been in the ICU at the time of the arrest!

But Nissi's life was in deep peril. At that time, ECMO was only used at a handful of pediatric hospitals across the country, and at many of those, they wouldn't even attempt to hook up a child with a single ven-tricle to an ECMO pump, due to the low rates of success. From a medical standpoint, even with him on ECMO, the odds were once again stacked heavily against us.

During all this chaos, we were blissfully snoozing at home. Carly demanded that someone else call us; this had been her first Code Blue in her young career, and she wanted nothing to do with our terrified reaction. And so it was that a doctor called us at close to 3:00 a.m. As soon as the phone rang, I leaped up. Even before my eyes were open, I was filled from head to toe with a feeling of cold dread. I somehow sensed, I *knew*, the call was bearing terrible news. And sure enough, the doctor on the line said, "Is this Nesanel's dad? Your son went into car-diac arrest. We're doing chest compressions on him right now. You and your wife need to come to the hospital. How soon can you get here?"

I stumbled back and forth in the room as we struggled to put on some clothes and wrap our heads around the news. Luckily, our downstairs tenant had babysat that evening, so I called her again and asked her to come back upstairs. She willingly agreed, going back to sleep on our living room couch until we'd return.

We drove through every red light on the empty streets in a mad dash to get to the hospital. I don't recall any tears, just intense, intense dread. But as we were running up the stairs from the parking lot, I told Chaya, "This *can't* be the end! We have too many mitzvos, too much goodness invested in him! G-d *cannot* finish it off here—it would be a desecration of His Name!"

The security guards had already been alerted of our impending arrival, so the doors were wide open for us—not locked, as they usually are at night. We ran briskly down the long, dark, silent hallway, all the way back to the ICU. The CICU was overloaded with patients, so we were directed to a room in the Pediatric ICU (PICU) just next door. In that single room, alone among the dozens of ICU rooms, the lights were glaring; the room was packed with personnel. Someone asked us if we wanted to be in the room. I responded, "Absolutely not! You do what you need to, and we won't get in your way." So she led us to the Quiet Room at the end of the PICU, where we were left in silent tears.

We said *Tehillim* in quiet urgency. But after about ten minutes, Chaya had enough of the dark loneliness, her maternal instinct screaming at her to be in close proximity to her baby, so we went back into the hall. Upon seeing us standing against the wall, wanting to be nearby but not in the center of the frenetic activity, a nurse thoughtfully put us in an empty room next to where they were working on Nissi. We sat down again heavily.

At about this point, I pulled out my phone to ask—or, rather, plead with—the people on my Facebook and WhatsApp groups who were following our story to say *Tehillim*. As I posted the request, I noticed a message had arrived in my inbox. It was from a girl I had met briefly some two or three years earlier. Her father was Jewish, and her mother was not. When we met, I told her that if she considered herself Jewish,

she should look into a proper conversion. The astounding message that
came in that night read:

> *Shalom Rabbi, I'm not sure if you remember me. You came to
> my house maybe a year or two ago on Purim to reach out to
> my family after seeing a menorah in the window. My father is
> Jewish, and my mother is technically not. Thank you for reach-
> ing out because it gave me strength to pursue an Orthodox
> conversion in Israel. I finished my conversion one month ago.
> I am saying Tehillim for your baby from Israel. May Hashem be
> with you and your family. I am praying for your child.*

I was awestruck at the turn of events from that seemingly insignifi-
cant, two-minute conversation. Even more, the timing of her message
filled me with hope. We weren't fighting this battle alone!

But there was another message—from Above—awaiting me on
Facebook. Facebook's algorithms, which usually fill my news feed with
useless information from people I barely even know, caused a second
message to appear on the small screen in front of me.

Reuven Sutin was a former college student at the University of
Pittsburgh. I'd met him many years earlier, when I was a young rabbin-
ical student, but I'd had little to do with him since moving to Seattle.
Early that morning (on the East Coast) he had posted on my father's
Facebook wall. He wrote the following: "I just saw Rafi in a dream. He
said the miracle happened because he has extraordinary parents."

My jaw dropped! Rafi, of course, was my older brother, who had died
of cystic fibrosis in 1997. Reuven had never even met him in person,
and certainly had no idea what we were going through at the moment
he posted the message. I showed these two messages to Chaya and told
her, "I'm sure he'll be fine. Messages like these don't just appear at
a time like this for no reason."

At the worst of moments, we were handed strands of hope. And I was
quite relieved to be leaning on the merits of my extraordinary parents.

Soon afterward, a nurse came in and said, "Everything's stable. You
can go see him now!" We entered the room. Nissi lay on the bed, looking

wan and still. More tubes and wires than ever protruded from his little body. But he was alive, and that's all that counted, even if he was leaning heavily on machines to keep him on this earth.

Eerie calm filled the room. The doctor came over to us and explained what they assumed had happened: The BT shunt, which had been positioned during his first surgery to allow blood flow between his heart and lung, had presumably clotted, causing a cardiac arrest. The plan was to send him to the "cath lab" soon for a catheterization to open up the clotted shunt. The catheterization included putting a wire stent into the shunt, which would crush the clot and hold the shunt open. Space had been made for him in the CICU, so he'd be moved there after the procedure.

Taking a deep breath, we signed the consent forms, tried to think of some sensible questions to ask, and looked lovingly at our little boy. We tiptoed over, carefully stepping around the many wires and tubes strewn across the room, and upon finding a spot of skin not covered with tape or attached to a device, touched his small hand in an attempt to transfer as much love and strength as we could. "We love you, Nissi. We're with you!" we whispered, and quietly left the room.

Considering that at this point everything was as under control as possible and Nissi was about to be sent to the cath lab, we decided it was time for us to get back home, relieve the babysitter sleeping on the couch, and get the kids off to school.

But before we went home, we had one more stop to make. We headed back to the post-surgical floor to update Carly and thank her. But how can you possibly thank someone who saved your child's life?! We obviously had to try, even though we knew that no words could ever possibly express our feelings of appreciation.

Carly was deeply touched by our sudden appearance and appreciative of the update. She admitted to us that she had been quite distraught after the crisis and had called her own mother for some emotional support. Hearing that Nissi was still alive and relatively stable filled her with relief. It was then that she told us about the incredible timing of the empty milk bag, which had caused the nurse to come into the room at the moment the shunt began clotting, the nurse's quick thinking, and the respiratory therapist who just "happened to be" next door. We were utterly speechless when it was revealed to us how G-d's Hand had been involved in every detail.

On our way out of the unit, we also noticed the father of the little boy who'd been Nissi's roommate. He was likewise relieved at the somewhat positive update and expressed his best wishes for Nissi. At about 6:30 a.m., we arrived back home. What a night it had been.

Chapter 5

Black and Blue

The older kids were told briefly that Nissi was back in the CICU. There was no reason to freak them out more than necessary, and like always, they took it in stride. Yehuda hadn't liked the more outdated decor of the post-surgical floor anyway. We drove the kids to school and went straight back to the hospital.

Our walk down the corridor to Nissi's new room in the CICU felt like a walk of shame. All our friends, the nurses who had been part of our journey, whether directly working with Nissi or just cheering us on, stood in front of their assigned rooms, shaking their heads sympathetically. As we passed through this gauntlet of sadness, I just muttered aloud, quoting my father, "Moving onward and upward!"

Nissi was now in the last bed space on the right, situated in the large, open suite nicknamed "The Naughty Room." With immediate proximity to the doctors' station and plenty of space, it was used for the sickest kids, the "naughty" ones who were in need of lots of equipment.

We walked into the room with bated breath. Nissi was lying still, with tubes, monitors, and wires everywhere. Two nurses were assigned to him, one exclusively for the ECMO machine. Two towering IV poles stacked with multiple medications stood over his bed. Doctors were constantly poking their heads in to look at another number or ask for another test result. Despite this, small semblances of familiarity stood out—his blanket, pictures drawn by his siblings, familiar music playing on our iPad, and a stuffed animal helped soothe the atmosphere.

Suzanne, an older nurse originally from New Zealand, was manning the ECMO machine, a position we nicknamed the "Techmo." The ECMO machine needed constant vigilance to ensure that the tubes would not suck up a clot and shoot it catastrophically into the heart or brain. Using a flashlight, she would carefully inspect the tubing for any particles or air bubbles. ECMO is simultaneously life-saving and deathly dangerous, so we were all hoping that he would only need it for a very short amount of time. Little did we know that it was as much a roll of the dice as anything else. Single-ventricle kids oftentimes don't do well with ECMO, but this was the only tool the doctors had available to give his heart and lungs a break and allow them time to heal.

PRIMARY ON OUR MINDS at this point was the question of neurological damage due to a lack of oxygen during the cardiac arrest. Nissi had EEG monitors stuck all over his head to watch for abnormalities in his brain function. He also had a partial lung collapse, and his lactate had soared once again, posting a twenty on a scale that only read that high. And his one and only valve in his heart, his common valve, had moderate regurgitation—meaning the valve flaps were not getting a tight grip as they closed, creating even more work for the heart to circulate blood. Things were tense, and it seemed like every update from the nurses was regarding another of his systems experiencing major trouble. This cardiac arrest wasn't a small bump in the road.

The fellow on call had a wholly mechanical attitude toward his patients. During rounds that first day, we were trying our best to process all the new information, working on very little sleep coupled with extreme stress. In the middle of giving his reports during rounds, his beeper went off. He pulled it off his belt, glanced at it, and said, "Oh, that was neurology. They want to be kept updated on his seizures."

Chaya and I felt like we'd been hit by a truck. Seizures?! We hadn't yet heard anything about seizures! With further clarification, it turned out that Nissi had only experienced two recorded subclinical seizures, which means that they did not express themselves anywhere externally, just inside the brain. He was put on Keppra, an anti-seizure medication, as a preventative measure. But this fellow's nonchalant attitude and insensitive manner of delivering bombshell information caused us to ask that he be removed from our case. Things were too stressful for us to have to deal with a callous young doctor, and by this time, we were confident enough in our dealings with the staff to request changes when we felt them necessary. Dr. Banker was understanding, and the fellow was quickly swapped out for a different one.

Our new medical fellow was Dr. Cara Von Zychlin, a caring and communicative professional. We developed a great relationship with her, and often, when she had free time, she'd come over to Nissi's room to talk. In one such conversation, the topic of hospital experiences came up, and I offhandedly mentioned that I'd had a brother with CF, which had given me a lot of experience in hospitals as a child. She gave me a funny look and asked if she could sit down and talk with us later. Knowing that it's never a good thing when the doctor wants to talk to you in private, we were understandably nervous.

A little while later, she sat down gently next to us. We spoke a bit about family, but all the while, we nervously wondered what she really wanted to talk about. After a few uncomfortable moments, she finally broke the tension and said, "You know, we just got back some of the birth screening results, and Nissi came back positive for cystic fibrosis."

I let out an audible sigh of relief, and said, "Oh, thank G-d, it's just CF!"

Until this point, we had seemed like fairly sensible parents, but our reaction to the news that our critically ill son might have another deadly disease had Cara looking at us dumbfounded. I met her confused look and laughed, "That will be the only time in your career you'll hear that sentence!"

We then proceeded to explain that we had been tested for genetic compatibility before we'd gotten married, and despite that, one of our children had come back from his birth screening positive for CF as well. We were terrified, until a sweat test a week later revealed it to be a false positive. I was sure this was the same scenario with Nissi. "There is no way his lungs could have handled the kind of abuse they just endured if he would have CF!" I told her. She agreed in theory but was insistent that he get the sweat test to confirm. A few months later, our suspicion was proven correct; thank G-d, Nissi did not have CF.

IN ANY CASE, things were still very much touch and go. A lung lobe collapsed again and needed to be reinflated. The X-ray revealed that his lungs were wet and full of fluid, so we monitored his urine output seriously as they tried to get that under control. His lactate was critically high. His heart valve leaking was indicative of significant trauma to the heart. His brain activity was monitored constantly, keeping alert for seizures. With all that going on, the first attempt to get him off ECMO—on day two after the cardiac arrest—failed.

Dr. Banker understood our stress well and didn't hesitate to come over and talk to us. She calmed our nerves significantly when she told us an anecdote that had happened early in her career. A child pulled a TV off a shelf, and it crushed her head. The doctors told the parents she would never walk or talk. Yet two years later, she walked into the ICU, a regular preschooler. "Kids are so resilient," she cautiously encouraged us. "The passageways in their brains have so much plasticity. They figure out ways to compensate." That story, and that conversation, gave us tremendous hope.

In the late afternoon a day later, our "Techmo," Suzanne, sent us a text message that buoyed our hopes even more. It read: "Just wanted to let you know…Your son is responding to touches, trying to open his eyes, and moving his limbs…" Seldom had a text message ever been more reassuring.

During this rough patch, Dr. Musa, an Ethiopian intensivist of international repute, said to us, "I was thinking about your son, and he reminds me of Moses, baby Moses in the basket, struggling for life…" That heartfelt sentiment was deeply appreciated.

We felt like the entire team was rooting us on. A nurse practitioner with whom we had little contact told us that she had dreamed of Nissi one night, dreaming that she saw him and all his siblings running down the street near her mother's house toward the local synagogue, Shaarei Tefillah.

By day three of ECMO, his lactate had dropped considerably, and they managed to keep the lung lobe inflated. We celebrated several other milestones as well: a clean brain scan, and, toward evening, he was successfully taken off ECMO. He had also reached a newfound status—that of a *bar kayama*, a halachically viable life, which is marked when a child reaches thirty days old. And that was how we celebrated his one-month birthday—in shock that he'd gotten that far, but in deep prayer that he'd keep going.

On March 10, his chest was closed once again, thankfully moving us away from the ECMO saga.

Things seemed like they were starting to look upward once again, but an extremely worrisome trend began exhibiting itself. Nissi's oxygen sats would suddenly drop like an anvil, a situation known as "desatting." Simply put, at even the slightest provocation he would go from steady breathing to not being able to absorb oxygen at all in mere seconds. He'd turn shades of deep eggplant purple from getting suctioned or being disturbed in any way. Figuring that it was due to the fragility of his general state, the nurses began keeping shots of heavy narcotics—morphine and Dilaudid—handy, since he'd desat on a dime and drop to incredible shades of blue and even gray.

Watching these desats was just about as freaky as things could get for a parent. His eyes would close tightly, and his color would deepen sickeningly. A glance at the oxygen saturation monitor showed the numbers cratering, and I remember telling him out loud, "C'mon, kid! Pull yourself together!" The nurses, as concerned as we were, would immediately shoot him up with the heaviest narcotics available, in the hopes that pain relievers would settle things.

Worriedly, we watched for some positive progression on those lines, but to no avail.

A WEEK AFTER THE ARREST, an early morning echocardiogram showed some slight improvement in the valve leakage. With that good news, we were hoping that his awful bouts of desatting would resolve themselves. But an early afternoon X-ray of his abdomen caused our hardy nurse, Maury, and Dr. Cara to audibly swear in frustrated exasperation.

"What's wrong now?" we asked. Cara looked upset. "He's got free air in his abdomen," she told us, deep concern evident on her face. "I was afraid of this...It means that his intestines perforated as a result of the cardiac arrest. The heart shuttled blood only to the vital organs, and the gut did not receive proper blood flow, causing damage. This must be dealt with immediately."

A GI surgeon, Dr. Avansino, was already on his way to us. After a very brief consultation with the team, and within a few short minutes, we were already being handed surgery-consent papers for signing. Dr. Avansino was crystal clear about his plans for the emergency surgery. "We're going to take out his intestine and inspect it for holes. We'll have to remove any dead tissue and give him an ostomy—artificial bags for his waste—and his abdomen will remain open for about three months until we'll be able to close it again."

Chaya and I were shocked at the immediacy and severity of the situation. "He's so fragile! Can we wait? And that plan sounds so extreme! Is there any chance you'll be able to sew his abdomen back up?" Dr. Avansino laughed sadly. "I'm afraid not. This is an urgent matter, and I can't see any way I'd be able to close him up. Frankly, it would be irresponsible if we did so, due to infections that could set in."

We signed the papers, and fearfully, we watched them get ready to whisk him away—yet again. Maury, sensing the absolute dread we felt sending him off to yet another major surgery just days after getting off ECMO, kindly told Chaya, "Go ahead, you can give him a hug." Chaya bent over the bed, talking softly to her little baby, arms cradling his body, afraid this would be the last time she'd see him alive. Maury watched and gently squeezed her shoulder, sharing her pain and trying to give over some reassurance. A final kiss, and Nissi was off. Desperately, I instructed the surgeon yet again to ask the surgical team to take on positive resolutions before they began the operation, and again, he wholeheartedly agreed to do so.

The three-hour surgery went by painfully slowly, and we tried to focus on saying *Tehillim*. Once more, we put out a call on social media for urgent prayers, and the troops were rallied. We were not alone, but we were on pins and needles...and when Nurse Maury finally came out with some news, we virtually jumped on her.

"Everything went well! Even better than expected!" she happily told us, but no other details were forthcoming quite yet. She told us the surgeon would meet us in the NICU to give us a full report, so we ran off to the waiting room next to the NICU to hear what he had to say.

Edgy as we were, it seemed like he was taking forever to get there. I paced back and forth impatiently. Suddenly, Dr. Avansino walked in briskly, throwing open the swinging doors like a gunslinger, with a silly, perplexed grin on his face. "It was his *appendix*!" he called out with evident shock. "When does *that* happen to a baby?!"[1]

The appendix is a very small organ that sits in middle of the intestine and makes very little difference to the body. It can be removed in a routine and fairly common operation. Hearing that the only hole in the entire intestine was in the appendix *and nowhere else* was phenomenal—and quite shocking given the medical circumstances.

As we tried to come to grips with this incredible news, I suggested that perhaps there had been a lack of blood flow to the appendix, which would explain why it ruptured. He shook his head vigorously. "That wouldn't make any sense—the appendix is smack in the middle of the intestine, and had there been a lack of blood flow, it would have affected—and ruptured—the intestine as well! We went through his entire intestine, inspected it centimeter by centimeter. While the color wasn't great—no surprise there, after all, he just had cardiac arrest—his intestines were clean, no holes! We were able to remove his appendix, close him up, and everything's great; he'll heal very quickly now!"

He also informed us happily that Nissi's intestines were not malrotated, as had been suspected by Dr. Ralph, and noted offhandedly that he saw no evidence of a spleen,[2] which clarified for us those questions.

We danced back to the CICU, and upon seeing some of our old nurse friends currently taking care of other patients, we eagerly shared with them the good news. Becky, one of the charge nurses, gushed, "That's a best-case scenario that wasn't even on my list!" Caitlin, a favorite nurse of Nissi's, was likewise shocked. "Appendix—that's a joke!" Incredulous, and ever so thankful, we looked forward to seeing things settle down once again.

---

1   Incredibly, much later, Dr. Emily told us, "Nissi saved another baby!" One of her patients in the PICU had similar symptoms, and she suggested, based on her memory of this case and to the utter surprise of her team, that it might be the appendix. Shockingly, it was...

2   The spleen is an organ that is central to the immune system. To counteract this, Nissi would be prescribed amoxicillin indefinitely.

BUT THINGS DIDN'T SETTLE DOWN QUICKLY. He remained in an ultra-precarious state, scaring the dickens out of anyone who had to treat him. He'd cough and immediately desat to the fifties and even lower. The lowest we saw at some point in this period was 17 percent—low enough to lose consciousness. We wondered if he was struggling with the ventilator tubes, placed hurriedly in his mouth while in the rush to get him onto ECMO instead of through the nose, a relatively more comfortable position. Or perhaps he was getting frustrated with the uncomfortable placement.

But the team was stuck between a rock and a hard place. Removal of the ventilator tube could be fatal if he wasn't ready for it. So in the meantime, the game plan was unchanged; keep the room dark, quiet, and try not to touch him. And when he goes blueberry colored, grab the narcotics—quick!

Kim, an African American nurse from Georgia with an infectious sense of humor, had us cracking up in laughter despite ourselves when giving us an update on his latest desat episode. Describing his incredibly low oxygen level and the deep, dark color he turned, she joked, "I was talking to your son. I said, 'Nissi, this color looks good on me—not on you!'" She also told us, "You know, I was thinking. Your son is either gonna be a total slacker or a CEO. There's no middle of the road for him!"

At some point, an X-ray revealed that his ventilator tube was placed rather deep in his chest, and an order was made to have it raised. The respiratory team worked gingerly around him, fearful of his fits. When no progress was made on the desat episodes, the team analyzed the latest X-rays in detail and noticed something startling. The ventilator tube was resting on his carina, which is the top of the lung and the location of the cough reflex! So *that* was why he was so touchy. I think having a tube sitting in that location would cause *any* of us to go blue! After that was clarified and the team carefully pulled the tube back up a millimeter or two, the poor baby finally began to rest a bit more easily.

A few days later, the ventilator was successfully moved from his mouth to his nose, a far more comfortable configuration, and a good sign that the team thought he was moving in the right direction. His blood work still showed signs of inflammation in his body, but eventually, these too began to look better, little by little.

Still, with all the slow going, ICU intensivist Dr. Mazer expressed worry in rounds one evening. "We'd expect him to be doing better," he said. "Typical recovery of an appendectomy is faster." I wasn't having any of it and interrupted him. "Dr. Mazer, when has *anything* this baby done been typical?!" He laughed, and agreed to hold off on the fear, and by extension, any new procedures or tests.

In fact, by March 18, he was stable enough that we were finally able to hold him for the first time since the cardiac arrest. Holding the little critter was a full team procedure, as he was attached to so many tubes that it took quite a bit of strategy to get him to a spot that was comfortable for both momma and baby, as well as the medical team. But the smile on Chaya's face, and the calm, relaxed look on Nissi's, made all the effort well worth it.

DURING ALL THIS TIME, we were getting more actively involved in the medical discussions, and even contributing to the direction the team was taking. At one point, we had noticed his NIRS numbers, which measure blood flow near the brain and kidneys, ominously trending downward, and suggested during rounds that perhaps it was due to needing blood, as his hematocrit was low. The doctors thought that to be a reasonable idea, so they ordered a transfusion—and voilà! His NIRS numbers spiked back up! This became a running suggestion of ours during rounds—asking, "What's his 'crit like?" It felt great for us to be a real partner in the process of his healing and gave us confidence in our understanding of the medical underpinnings.

Toward the holiday of Purim, things were calm enough to run a few trials on CPAP (continuous positive airway pressure), a ventilator that applies mild air pressure on a continuous basis, creating a bridge between full breathing support and breathing on his own with extra oxygen support. Day by day, they increased his workload, and by Purim, he was completely on the lowest setting of CPAP and almost ready for being extubated. A few very rough days knocked back that schedule, but on March 27, his face finally reappeared in full view as the ventilator was removed, and, as a bonus, his chest stitches were taken out.

Now the goals were clear once again: start feeds, get completely off oxygen, wean him off the narcotics, and get off the blood pressure medication. On the twenty-eighth, Nissi was finally visited by his siblings again, and on the twenty-ninth, we bid a happy farewell to the Naughty Room and were greeted by the spectacular view of the snow-capped fourteen-thousand-foot Mt. Rainier in our new suite. Springtime seemed to be well on its way, even if we weren't much part of it.

Chapter 6

Bounce Back

Over the next two weeks, things were mostly faring well. Nissi finally began taking feeds by mouth again and was being weaned off medication by medication. Small issues cropped up here and there—after all, life couldn't get too boring in Nissi's world! His stools showed traces of blood, which kept the doctors worried and slightly puzzled. But nothing ever came of that, and by the time we crawled to his two-month birthday, we even got a smile. Or maybe it was a grimace. But it was good, whatever it was.

A little note on Nissi's personality: During his first week of life, he showed himself to be very calm. He only cried when he needed to be fed, and was easily consolable. I was convinced that this was his real personality, although I assure you that during his blue episodes the nurses thought he had the anger of the Incredible Hulk himself. They laughed off any of my comments to the contrary. But as he began healing, he'd break into cheeky smiles that lit up the room.

On April 11, we finally found ourselves heading back to the post-surgical floor. We were good and ready for this moment, although maybe Nissi wasn't. He had a meltdown smack in the middle of the transport, which resulted in one very dirty diaper that needed to be changed mid-hallway. After changing the diaper and calming the rascal, we continued on our way.

I put in a personal plea with the nurses to not put us in the same room we'd been in for his cardiac arrest, as we had a fair amount of PTSD remaining from that unpleasant experience. They assented and gave us a room with no roommates, directly across from the nurses' station, providing him pretty tight care for the rest of his stay. He was still on the high-flow ventilator via nasal prongs, but that was just so that we wouldn't need to send him back to the ICU if he needed some help. And, in fact, within a few days on the floor, out they went.

By April 14, Nissi's IV pump was shut down at last. What a sight! It was so beautiful to see the stark change from what had been a veritable forest attached to him—several poles attached to machines dispensing medications piled four wide and three tiers high—to just a single remaining pole sitting dark and lifeless in the corner of the room, out of an abundance of caution in case it was needed. Now, all that he was attached to was the monitoring equipment and his NG tube.

As Passover approached, we began discussing with the doctors the idea of going home. "Look, we'll be thrilled to take him home at any time—but let's try not to make it on the eve of Passover!" we pleaded, to the incredulous looks of the doctors. The thought of bringing home a complex baby on the busiest day of the Jewish year, with the myriad tasks and responsibilities of the baby on top of the infinite minutia of the holiday, was enough to give us fits. But there was yet more healing to be done, and Passover arrived with Nissi still in the hospital.

BY NOW, poor Nissi's body had expressed displeasure with every organ system besides one: the liver. Not one to leave things unfinished, Nissi duly started turning yellow, a new color for him. Upon reporting this to the nurses, we were told they'd take an hour-long ultrasound to check things out. Chaya went with them to radiology to keep him calm during the procedure. But things started to get nerve-racking. The supposed one-hour procedure ended up taking close to three, and no one was giving Chaya any information. She returned to the post-surgical floor with him, her nerves shot, and we waited impatiently for the liver doctor, a hepatologist, to arrive.

The hepatologist only showed up after several hours of our waiting, and by the time she came, two worried parents were an anxious mess. To be clear, logic dictated to us that all was fine, but we desperately wanted to be assured of that. However, the lengthy ultrasound coupled with no information other than "The doctor will come up to talk to you!" was not exactly a balm to those nerves. When the long-awaited doctor finally came to Nissi's room, she peppered us with questions. What color was his stool? How long had he been yellow? I pulled out my phone, and we were able to compare pictures to answer those questions. It had only been several days.

"I'm worried about liver atresia," the doctor finally said, and she described an extremely ill baby with many side effects, such as white stool.

"But he doesn't have any of those symptoms!" I cried out in exasperation.

"You're right," she replied. "We're pretty sure he's fine and just has high bilirubin from being on an IV for two months straight. But we want to make sure it's not liver atresia. We'll keep an eye on things."

I was just about ready to explode from frustration, although I held my tongue. What I wanted to say was, "C'mon, doc! Why couldn't you calm us first with the expectation that everything was, for all intents and purposes, probably fine, and only afterward discuss a worst-case scenario?"

This was a classic example of how all too many doctors toss families into unnecessary emotional trauma. As I posted on Facebook, "Are your tenterhooks kosher for Passover? Mine are!"

It turns out that the ultrasound took so long because the ultrasound technicians struggled to follow his veins to his liver, due to his unique anatomy. But they weren't allowed to tell us that because of puerile medical information rules. Perhaps if someone had been sensitive enough to give us even the slightest bit of information, our nerves wouldn't have been on the verge of snapping. Ridiculous!

LITTLE BY LITTLE, Nissi began to gain weight. Things were coming along swimmingly, with home just a day away, when we noticed some slight changes one Saturday night. A slight fever, tachypnea (fast breathing), and higher-than-usual heart rate. As a precaution, we were sent right back to the ICU. While there, they put him back on the high-flow oxygen—and boy, was he furious at that! Turns out that our old friend the hematocrit was low, and one transfusion was enough to get him stabilized. It did result in some frustration with a nurse who had played by the book and hadn't taken us seriously when we'd pointed those details out on Saturday night, but within forty-eight hours, he was back on the post-surgical floor.

Coming from the high-intensity medical care and easy access to the doctors in the CICU, the relatively laissez-faire world of the post-surgical floor drove us crazy. We felt that the residents were simply not qualified to deal with a kid as medically complicated as Nissi. One resident, after seeming unsure about how to remove Nissi's shirt, looked at his stomach scar and asked, "Is that where they took his appendix out?"

Chaya looked at him in shock—where did he think they took his appendix from?! (It was only later that we learned that his wasn't a typical appendectomy scar—his was a full-scale intestinal surgery scar—and not the small mark left from a laparoscopic surgery. But the resident's somewhat clueless comment kept us on edge.)

It would take some time before we'd finally understand the system the post-surgical floor runs on. Eventually, we came to appreciate the residents who would, in a nod to recognizing their own youthful inexperience, introduce themselves as "student doctors, here to learn." The self-acknowledgment of their student status gave us confidence that they would not overstep their knowledge.

THE CASE CARDIOLOGIST we were working with now was eager to get us out the door, and we were excited to leave as well. We concluded Passover with an emotional Mashiach's Meal at which we made hearty toasts to Nissi's arrival home, and he was finally released from the hospital the very next morning.

Our minivan was packed to the brim with supplies; it seemed there was barely enough room for the baby. While no confetti papered our drive home, we were certainly in a party mood. Finally, finally home! We had all been through so much to get to this point, and we were finally once again one family under the same roof. Nissi's siblings rejoiced at his arrival, eager to give him his pacifier, hold him, and bring him toys, but he looked on in terrified consternation. We began to unload the boxes of equipment we'd been given that would now grace our bedroom. Now the awesome responsibility of the nurses was on us; we had a bucketload of drugs to administer every few hours.

With everything pretty much organized, we settled down to what would be an insane night. We'd been given an iPad to record his oxygen sats, a brand-new technology only recently developed, but it refused to work. The anklet monitoring his vitals kept slipping off, setting off the alarm and keeping us and the kids awake. And the medication schedule called for 11:00 p.m., 12:00 a.m., and 5:00 a.m. doses. Sleep would only come in short, fitful intervals, if at all.

When morning dawned, a cranky baby awoke to his completely bushed parents. At about 11:00 a.m., a homecare nurse arrived. To our shock, it was the same woman who'd come to sign us in to hospice care when we'd brought Nissi home the first time! I laughingly apologized for asking her not to come back, and I asked her what her reaction had been when I'd informed her that we'd been admitted to Seattle Children's for surgery. As she answered, her voice caught. "To be honest," she said, "I was driving then, and I almost drove off the road! I actually had to pull over to the side of the road to catch my breath," she recalled.

But she was also not happy at Nissi's current state of affairs. His heart rate and breathing were too fast for her liking. We tried to attribute it to his drug schedule. The heavy narcotic Dilaudid created a druggie's hankering as his system awaited each kick. She hung around for an extra two hours to see what would happen after those heavier drugs were administered. But things didn't get better at all. And after a few phone calls, she firmly suggested, or, rather, insisted, that we head to the emergency room, confirming her opinion with Dr. Files, Nissi's outpatient cardiologist. Feeling deflated, we packed Nissi up again and headed back to the hospital.

At the ER, the eternally bow-tied Dr. McQuinn assessed things. To be frank, he was furious and frustrated at the previous cardiologist for releasing us while Nissi was still not perfectly stable, and upset at the pharmacists for giving us an impossible medication schedule. The paperwork was submitted to readmit Nissi to the CICU. Swallowing our disappointment, we steadied ourselves for the next round. We realized the mistake we'd made: we had set our sights on the wrong goals. We'd been so hyper-focused on getting him home that we'd forgotten what *he* needed—Nissi needed the "Glenn."

THE GLENN PROCEDURE is the second in the series of three surgical fixes for a child with a single ventricle. During this surgery, they'd reroute his blood circulation and eliminate the BT shunt. The superior vena cava (which brings blood back from the upper part of the body) would be disconnected from the heart and connected directly to the pulmonary artery. This surgery allows the single ventricle anatomy to supply oxygenated blood to the body in a much more stable fashion. Typically, it's performed at about five to six months and when the baby's weight is upward of 11 pounds (5 kilograms). Nissi was at 10.2 pounds (4.6 kilograms) and nearing his three-month birthday, which was the very earliest they'd be willing to do the surgery, so we changed tack. What would it take to get him to the Glenn?

For now, he was a quiet patient in the CICU, a lovely change of pace. X-rays and echocardiograms revealed nothing concerning, and on the morning of May 9, he underwent his second catheterization, measuring his internal blood pressures and getting precise imaging. Everything looked good, although that pesky shunt showed some narrowing due to possible clotting. This made the Glenn a necessity sooner rather than later, and a surgical conference was called to get a full team perspective.

As things had somewhat calmed on the cardiac lane, Nissi's strange gastrointestinal system became a bigger concern. Doctors differed on what they were seeing on film. Did he have a large esophagus and tiny stomach? Or did his stomach herniate upward into his chest? Did he have or didn't he have a hernia? The question was whether or not he'd be in danger of choking when eating or as a result of reflux, and if this needed to be dealt with more urgently than the cardiac issues. One potential stomach fix was the Nissen fundoplication, in which the stomach would be pinned or tied around the esophagus. One of the fellows was dead set on Nissi needing the Nissen, which Chaya quickly deemed ridiculously invasive. This resulted in an underlying tiff between us. But at a surgical conference, the GI team would meet with the cardiac team and the surgeons to bandy about ideas.

More dilemmas surfaced due to these discussions, specifically in the area of feeding. Up until this point, Nissi had been receiving the majority of his food and nutrition via a feeding pump. There are four different ways to get the milk from the bag to his stomach: the naso-gastric (NG) tube, the naso-duodenum (ND) tube, the gastric (G) tube, or gastro-jejunal (GJ) tube. The difference between them is the level of access each one provides to the stomach or gut. The NG tube, which we'd been using until now, goes from the nose to the stomach, while the ND tube goes all the way to the gut; the G-tube is surgically placed directly into the stomach, and the GJ tube includes an extension that reaches into the intestine.

The question at this point was whether or not sending food deeper into the gut or intestine would help his reflux and make things easier for him. Under consideration were the advantages and disadvantages of the different mechanisms. The NG and ND tubes easily slip out, necessitating replacement—not a dangerous procedure, but an annoying one, particularly for the ND tube. Should we instead take the leap and send him into surgery to have a G-tube or GJ tube placed? Or should we avoid yet another surgery, at least for right now, especially if it was not crucial?

Dr. McQuinn attacked these issues with a multipronged approach, hoping something would stick and help Nissi's worsening reflux as well as his rapid breathing and high heart rate. First, he switched the NG tube for an ND tube. Nissi was already on every reflux medication available. He also introduced a proposed change from Dilaudid to methadone—a heavy narcotic typically used to help opiate addicts out of their addiction—in order to ease the effects of the withdrawal symptoms, hoping that was at least a partial culprit for the high heart rate. Sure enough, after applying these quick fixes, things settled down somewhat. However, we'd end up waiting quite a while before we'd finally get a long-term plan for his GI problems. (In fact, as of this writing, four years and several GI teams later, we're still waiting!)

On May 10, the medical teams met for the surgical conference, and afterward, Dr. McMullan came by to give us the plan. "We're moving ahead with the Glenn, either Friday or Monday," he told us.

We were curious as to the conversation at the conference. Dr. McMullan chuckled. "Everyone was worried because post-Glenn, ECMO isn't effective. So they were all tied up on that, in case he'd need ECMO at a future date. But I kept on muttering under my breath, 'What are you all worried about? The kid is indestructible!'"

Obviously, Chaya and I got quite a kick out of that comment! We prayed that he'd continue that way.

Nissi would pass one more milestone—and one more ridiculous incident—prior to his next surgery. We were visiting on Saturday night, and I innocently picked him up from his baby swing—and out slid his ND tube! It just slipped right out. Of course, I felt terrible, as NG tubes can be placed by anyone, but ND tubes need to be checked by X-ray to ensure they are placed correctly. They are also notoriously difficult to thread properly, not just down the nose into the stomach, but the technician needs to fish around while it is in the stomach, hoping to somehow feed it into the small hole at the bottom of the stomach that leads to the intestine. Nissi's wacky anatomy makes this even more complicated.

As they wheeled in the portable ultrasound to check the nurse's placement (he failed two tries before we left; another nurse would eventually succeed on the fifth go), I said, "I wonder how many X-rays and ultrasounds he's had?"

We peered at the screen, and what do you know? The one hundredth screenshot of his anatomy was next up! My idea of holding a massive celebration with streamers and balloons was shot down.

And as for the ND tube...well, just a few minutes before the nurse swapped out for the day shift, he peered in the room—only to see Nissi nonchalantly holding the tube in his little hand! He sighed, picked up the baby, and held him until his shift ended. He then passed Nissi and his troublesome ND tube off to the next shift.

Chapter 7

The Glenn

The ride to school the morning of May 16 was somewhat humorous, and touching, as the kids tried to grasp the fact that their brother was going to be operated on yet again. "I won't be able to concentrate!" Yehuda cried out from the back of the car. "I'll be thinking, *Now the doctor's holding my brother's heart!*" Shayna concurred and wondered what would happen if the surgeon dropped Nissi's heart.

We'd been warned by the nurses that post-Glenn babies have a whopper of a headache until their body gets used to the new pressures the fresh plumbing creates, so we were quite worried about what his reaction would be. He hadn't shown himself to be a quick healer, and we knew not to expect the typical seven to ten days for recovery. With apprehension of a possible upcoming roller coaster in mind, we took the family to a beach in Vancouver for a day, trying to fuel up for the ride ahead by drinking in the spectacular beauty of the Pacific Northwest.

We noticed a funny difference in the way the staff in the ICU related to the Glenn compared to the staff on the floor. Nurses in the regular unit often said, "Oh, we love our Glenn babies!" A few days before the Glenn, we mentioned that while in conversation with a nurse in the CICU, and she reacted in horror. "I don't know what they're talking about! Glenn babies are awful—they are cranky nonstop!" Well, apparently Glenns are great—only once they start healing and are able to leave the ICU!

Considering all the wild rides he'd gone on during his previous recuperation periods, we decided to do something extra to keep ourselves and the kids focused on the positive attitude we wanted to maintain.

The children made posters with messages we wanted to live with, to decorate his latest CICU room. Our little nine-year-old artist Naomi made a beautifully intricate, colorful poster with the words "Stay Positive!" adding a little yellow emoji with a gigantic, goofy smile.

On Monday afternoon, at 4:00 p.m., Nissi was wheeled away for the Glenn procedure, to be performed by our trusty surgeon, Dr. McMullan. He had actually planned out his surgical strategy for this procedure while operating on Nissi the first time around. And once again, he gladly agreed to ask the team to take on positive resolutions in Nissi's merit before the operation.

Thankfully, his recovery wasn't as bad as we thought it would be. It's possible that not much could top what we'd already seen. He expressed the notorious post-Glenn attitude as, more or less, "Hold me. Don't even *think* of putting me down. Especially if my narcotics are due." We were fine with that!

He was extubated just a day after surgery, and they were hoping to re-move the IV from his neck, where it had been placed due to the unique needs of the Glenn. It would be replaced by a fresh PICC line a few days later. This was faster than usual, because Nissi's superior vena cava, on which the Glenn circulation is dependent, is small, and they didn't want it doing any work but feeding blood to the heart.

The day after surgery was déjà vu—a small lung lobe collapse. They put him on the CPAP setting on the high-flow ventilator, and within a few days it reinflated. Now we were back in fairly familiar territory: wean him from the narcotics, lower the pressure on the oxygen tanks, and watch his sats.

It was with the latter of the three that Nissi, once again, threw every-one for a loop. His oxygen sats began wandering around the nineties, which to us looked great—an overachiever! Dr. Musa, however, ex-pressed bewilderment. "Glenn babies shouldn't have the physical ability to have oxygen saturations that high," she wondered aloud. The reason for this is because of the unique Glenn "plumbing" that allows the sin-gle ventricle to provide oxygenated blood to the entire body—only the upper body is receiving fully oxygenated blood, while the lower body receives a blend of oxygenated and non-oxygenated blood.

Determined to find the reason for it, she started reviewing his oft-photographed inner workings, going through his X-rays and ultrasounds in great detail. After significant effort, she finally found the culprit: two "new" veins called collaterals. These tiny veins could have been there since birth, or they could have been created by the body when the heart was under pressure from the cardiac arrest. Collaterals could cause problems if they siphon off blood that doesn't go anywhere useful, as this can cause the heart to work harder. Thankfully, these weren't causing any problems just yet, but we were told the team would keep an eye on them.

As for the narcotics, now that he was finally settling down post-op, we were ready to make the move from Dilaudid, a narcotic with heavy side effects during weaning, to methadone (which we called "meth" for short, eliciting some great reactions), which has a much more stable wean. At this point, we were all in for Dr. McQuinn's slow and steady approach, and encouraged the staff to heed to that plan of action.

It took close to two weeks before we were ready to get back down to the regular unit. For part of that time, we were considered to be in "floor" status while still in the ICU, a state that only someone with a history as legendary as Nissi could have—too healthy for the ICU, too unstable for the regular unit. It was also almost two weeks until we finally saw the poor kid crack a smile again. But as he got used to his body's new circulation, he began to relax, and finally, on June 1, we were sent back down the long corridor to the regular unit.

By this time, we'd finally "learned the system" on the post-surgical floor. We made sure that he'd have a single unit, placed directly in front of the nurse's station. In fact, at one point we even had the risk nurse as his private nurse for a period. We also met with anyone of power to make sure that the residents would not be running his care. While possibly offensive, at this point in the game, we knew we needed to trust our gut and stand up for what we felt was the best plan for Nissi. It just didn't make any sense that decisions for a kid with as many complications as Nissi should be made by someone who wasn't even allowed in the CICU! Thankfully, the staff understood our worries and tried to create a system that fit us.

Yet even as he slowly moved off the oxygen, had his chest stitches taken out (yet again), and dropped more narcotics, Nissi was loathe to keep things boring. A strange air bubble popped up in an unexpected place, which had everyone puzzled for a few days, until it began to subside. We believe it was escaped air from one of the chest tubes. And in one of his post-Glenn, headachy, angry episodes, he actually blew a gasket—the clot remaining from his neck IV popped and caused an ugly, bloody mess on the poor kid's neck. The gunky, grimy mess needed a visit from a wound specialist, and for at least a week, he had a powdered neck to add to his vast variety of treatments.

MEANWHILE, we were getting very frustrated from the lack of communication with the GI team. What was going on with his stomach, we wondered?! How were we progressing toward being released from the hospital when we had no idea what the diagnosis of his stomach issues were, let alone a game plan?

Requests to see the GI doctor as an inpatient were rebuffed. They sent us a resident once or twice, which led to more annoyance and confusion. After all our pushing and prodding, we finally got a surgical fellow to come by, and it ended up being someone who knew Nissi. Dr. Smith had seen us briefly during our first evening in the CICU to assess things from a general surgical point of view, and she'd also been present at his intestinal surgery. I asked her if she'd like to see Nissi's nicely healing scar, and she responded gladly. "Well, I sewed him up—I'd love to see it!"

Dr. Smith drew a diagram on the room's whiteboard and explained that his stomach and esophagus were really unique. In the imaging, one could not be differentiated from the other. We really wouldn't know what would happen until he grew. But as things were working just fine with the status quo of the ND tube, we'd just continue with that method of treatment until we saw a need for something else.

Slowly, we began to see the different medical specialties conflicting with each other. Our lovely physical therapist, Karen, was adamant that he'd need a G-tube, and was eager to get him moving with regular feeds. The GI team didn't want to do anything. And both of them looked at each other with rolling eyes. Honestly, after reflection, we were happy with the (lack of) course of action; we felt that he really needed to recuperate before undergoing any other surgical procedures. So even though we still couldn't define where his esophagus ended and stomach began, and whether or not he had a hernia...well, one doesn't need to know everything, I guess.

Finally, on June 14, the day after the holiday of Shavuos, we packed him up and happily left Seattle Children's Hospital yet again, hoping, yet pretty confident, that with a more stable child and a more stable medication schedule, this time it would last longer than eighteen hours.

Chapter 8

Tube-Tied

Having concluded five months with a baby in the hospital, we were more than ready for "normal" life. Sure, we had a calendar full of appointments with almost every "ology" that exists, but Nissi wasn't in the hospital anymore. No more nighttime or early-morning calls to check on the little gremlin. No more trying to juggle the competing demands of family life and hospital life. Finally, and with a medicine list that read like a daily review of the Stock Exchange, we were ready for some peace and tranquility.

All of his medications were being administered via his ND tube, which ran from his nose into his gut. You may recall that he was taken off the NG tube, which goes to the stomach, prior to the Glenn, as one of several measures they took to stabilize him. The assumption was that everything was working well, so no need for any changes.

A mere week after he got home, things started to go haywire. It began when we were uneventfully giving him his medications. The last medication of the group were his probiotics. And, to our surprise, the syringe stubbornly refused to push the liquid down the tube. Both Chaya and I tried our hand, with no success. Eventually, the pressure exerted just spurted goop out the valve on the side. We looked at each other in exasperation—now what?

Well, we knew that the ND tube can only be replaced by the pros, and proper placement can only be checked using X-rays. We'd been warned that ND's caused parents no end of grief and visits to the emergency room because of that, and it looked like we were headed that way. Waiting would do us no favors, since Nissi needed to be fed, so we packed up his stuff and drove to the ER.

At the ER, the staff tried their best to flush the tube (warm Coke was one quick fix suggested; who knew?!), but to no avail. That meant replacement time, and we were escorted from the ER to Interventional Radiology. After a six-hour experience with one extremely unhappy baby, which included a fluoroscopy and about an hour or two worth of constant X-rays to ascertain placement of the tricky tube, it was finally placed in the proper position, and Nissi was good to go.

The following Shabbos, it got stuffed up again. So off we marched back to the ER. And, once again, the poor screaming baby was strapped to the table while the doctors tried their best to feed the tube through his wacky anatomy. I tried to lighten the mood, singing quietly to him and cracking jokes with the staff. All the while, Nissi gripped Chaya's or my finger tightly, viselike. Thankfully, the staff appreciated my efforts and didn't throw me out of the room!

It was then that I came up with the idea for an epic rock number called "Heterotaxy Blues." Eventually, I actually wrote down some silly lyrics and gave the doctors a good laugh when I showed it to them:

> *I've got the heterotaxy blues*
> *My issues come in twos*
> *I'm among the rare fews*
> *Confounding the medical crews*
>
> *Where do I start*
> *I've got half a heart*
> *Got inner turmoil*
> *My guts backward coil*
>
> *I'm missing my spleen*
> *You know what I mean*
> *Everything's misplaced*
> *But it's not the worst I've faced*
>
> *I've replicated my right*
> *Yet nothing's in sight*
> *Twice my heart fire*
> *So long as it don't tire*

Through the nose goes my food
And the ND's misconstrued
When that tube comes out
Is when I really wanna shout

For I've got the heterotaxy blues
My issues come in twos
I'm among the rare fews
Confounding the medical crews.

High art it isn't, I'll admit to that. But it relieved the tension, and that was important.

It seemed like it took forever. We fretted about his blood pressure and oxygen sats, and Nissi screamed loud enough to wake the dead, turning all sorts of shades of red and violet while utilizing every bit of power his lungs could exert. We attempted various tactics to calm him—singing, holding his hand, talking to him—but nothing worked. Apparently, Nissi thought that having a plastic tube threaded down his nose into his gut while being forcibly restrained wasn't his idea of a picnic. Well, it wasn't ours either. But eventually they got the tube through to the right spot, and we were finally sent on our way. This time, though, we got an explanation for the stuffed tube: the probiotics were the culprit! They actually expand over time, and the remnants of each day's dose built up slowly in the tube, eventually blocking it completely. So we quickly eliminated them from his medication list.

Problem solved, right?

Not really. On the very next Friday afternoon, with Shabbos approaching, no less, he reached up and pulled the tube out of his nose! Completely exasperated, Chaya headed back to the ER, and I met her there, having zipped up the I-5 from Joint Base Lewis-McChord, where I'd been working that day. (The ER security guard looked at me in confusion. He'd now seen me three times in two weeks, so he certainly recognized my face. But the US Air Force uniform that followed my Chassidic Shabbos garb? That was a bit more than he could handle!) This time, we got the tube replaced in a snappy five hours and managed to get out of the hospital just before Shabbos.

Sunday was bright and beautiful. Perfect weather for a short hike, our first chance to really relax, baby in tow, after all those crazy months. After some brief research to find a quiet park with good views and a paved walking path for the stroller, we settled on the Bellevue Botanical Gardens. Enjoying the spectacular fresh air of the Pacific Northwest, we slowly pushed the stroller and watched Naomi, Levi, and Menachi run around with nary a care in the world. As we enjoyed the newfound calm and stillness, one of us stole a glance at the innocent-looking baby. His tube was hanging off his stroller, laughing at us, as the pump spat baby formula all over the ground in a white puddle.

Chaya and I looked at each other incredulously. Well, here we go again—back to the ER! Six more hours of torment for the poor baby, with pizza at a restaurant for dinner for the rest of the kids—and a fresh ND tube was in once again.

Until Monday morning. When he pulled the tube out. Again.

This time, the doctor in Interventional Radiology was having no success getting a new tube in, and being a bit sick of the game, he wasn't even trying too hard. Poor Nissi was already quite knowledgeable of the process, and we're pretty sure his fits of anger upon seeing the room set the whole hospital on edge. After nine attempts at getting the tube in the proper position, the doctor on call sent us upstairs to be admitted to the hospital so the ICU team would be able to get a dehydrated Nissi some fluids.

But when we got back to the post-surgical ward, there would be no success there either. Having missed some eight hours of feeds a day earlier, and another eight on Friday, his dehydration made putting an IV in even more difficult than usual. He'd always been a tough IV poke, even early on in his "career," and now his dry veins made things more difficult, rolling around in absolute rejection of the needle. The staff called their best IV people on him, to no avail. Everyone sat around totally perplexed.

It seemed that we were in real trouble. He was not proficient enough to eat alone, and his reflux was assumed to be too bad to have an NG tube instead of the ND tube, so the medical team gathered around to figure out the next step. The idea being bandied about was a surgical procedure to place a GJ tube instead, which eliminates the passage through the nose (the *n* in NG and ND) and just sets a little valve straight into the stomach and feeds directly into the intestine, as long as it could fit his anatomy. Chaya was not happy about this idea at all—she'd had enough of surgery and everything it entailed for now.

In the meantime, 6:00 p.m. was fast approaching, and his med schedule called for his narcotics to be administered then. Being that he was on methadone, it was crucial that we gave him his drugs on time so he wouldn't begin to react adversely from the drug wean, so I turned to the charge nurse with a flash of inspiration.

"As things stand right now, while we were unable to get the tube to reach the gut, the fact is that it's currently properly placed in his stomach. So why don't we try to give him his narcotics through it, and let's see what happens? If he throws it up, we'll know that the ND tube is the only choice. We'll have to put him under anesthesia to do it, and we can discuss an operation to place a GJ tube. But why not try using the NG tube, give him Pedialyte to get him hydrated, and see how it goes?"

The nurse thought that was a decent idea, ran it by the doctor, who concurred, and promptly gave him his drugs. An hour later, with no ill effects noticed, they began running feeds on a slow drip. By 9:00 p.m., the doctors informed us that if he kept up the serene attitude all night, he'd be released in the morning.

And so it was, rocking his snazzy new NG tube, Nissi went home. Life would prove to be a lot less eventful minus the ND tube and plus the NG tube, and Chaya would prove to be the stalwart replacer of slipped NG tubes.

Truth be told, Chaya was well on her way to earning her nursing degree. She took over the vast majority of the responsibilities, including one that was particularly difficult for me—a shot of Lovenox, a blood thinner, twice a day. The poor baby's thighs were covered in bruises, but Chaya soldiered on.

Those hypodermic needles caused some surreal moments—like pulling them out at a wedding or giving him his shots in an airport bathroom. But one unforgettable moment was when we woke up in the morning to find his crib sheets soaked in blood. When the initial shock wore off after a few seconds, we picked up the cooing and clueless baby, and with incredible relief, we realized nothing worse had happened other than we must have hit a vein during his most recent shot. Thin blood it sure was. We were very thankful when he was finally taken off Lovenox at the end of September.

Chapter 9

The Return of the Regurgitation

First results from cardiology post-hospitalization were great. Things were ticking along to the extent that Dr. Files thought he could let the leash out for Nissi to have three-month stints without being seen by a cardiologist.

But toward the end of July, things began to take a small slide downward. The much-spoken-about-but-little-done-about stomach seemed to be showing its colors, as Nissi began vomiting more and was acting pretty cranky. At his next visit, Dr. Files noticed more common valve regurgitation, which disturbed him. Considering that Nissi's oxygen sats began creeping once again into the nineties, which put an unnecessary workload on his heart, the likely culprit would be the extra collateral veins that had been detected after the Glenn. And with that in mind, Nissi headed back to the hospital for a brief catheterization, a one-day stay booked for August 15.

The catheterization went well. We learned that even more vein collaterals had grown in the interim period since they'd been identified by Dr. Musa. They were all capped off successfully, and his sats went back to where they were supposed to be, in the mid-80s. With things so much more stable, we began planning the event that had been on our minds for months—the *seudas hoda'ah*. It was time to express our thanks to G-d for everything we'd been through up until that point.

THE WHOLE COMMUNITY turned out for the event, as well as family and friends from out of town, filling the Shaarei Tefillah synagogue sanctuary from wall to wall. The full house was symbolic of what we felt had helped carry us through the difficult months: a communal cocoon of love and concern.

Our good friend Lily Stute helped us design little placards for all the tables. Each table card had the chapter of *Tehillim* corresponding to Nissi's age, chapter one, on one side, and a picture of him with a quote about miracles on the other side of the placard. Those quotes were taken from various places across classic Jewish sources. We wanted to illustrate our feeling of being totally overwhelmed by the miracles G-d had blessed us with. The best voice we could use toward that end was to quote the Torah itself—straight from the source.

We chose the following quotes:

- "A miracle involving sickness is greater than the miracle of Chananya, Mishael, and Azarya, who were saved from a fiery furnace. For the latter were saved from the effects of a human's fire, while the former is saved from the fire of Heaven."[1]
- "How many miracles does G-d perform for man of which man does not know?"[2]
- "There are miracles within nature and miracles beyond nature. Miracles hidden within nature come from a higher source, as they transcend both nature *and* the supernatural."[3]
- "Even if an unsheathed sword sits on a man's neck, he should not consider himself withheld from G-d's mercy."[4]
- "The Children of Israel said to the Al-mighty, 'It's Your job to perform miracles for us, and it's our job to praise and bless Your Name!'"[5]

---

1   *Nedarim* 41a.
2   *Shemos Rabbah* 24:1.
3   *Sefer HaMa'amarim Melukat* vol. 4, p. 225.
4   *Berachos* 10a.
5   *Bamidbar Rabbah* 19:20.

- "A miracle is a statement of the deepest truth: that nothing in existence is outside of G-d's unity."[6]

I asked my childhood friend Rabbi Binyamin Walters to fly out from Chicago to be our guest speaker at the celebration, and he spoke on the subject of Judaism's approach to the art of appreciation. The children led the crowd in the recitation of chapter one of *Tehillim* for Nissi, and I reviewed the story up to that point in its full glory for the first time publicly, culminating my speech with a list of the miracles we'd been blessed with, in the poetic style of the Passover Seder's *Dayeinu*:

- He survived birth.
- His PDA miraculously remained open for four days.
- He survived two open-heart surgeries, a stomach surgery, and three heart catheterizations.
- The pulmonary vein repair is notorious for having issues, yet his has been perfect.
- He survived cardiac arrest and fifty minutes of CPR without any major hit to his neurological system.
- He survived three days of ECMO with no negative results.
- He survived extremely dangerous oxygen desat episodes.
- When his intestines perforated, it was in the most curable spot possible.
- He's had no significant damage to any other organ system, despite injuries to every system at various points.
- His stomach issues aren't nearly as bad as originally thought. The original diagnosis was completely wrong.
- And, finally, no small miracle at all: friends fundraised a significant amount of money for us to live off of for these six months, and assisted us to get help in many, many ways.

I concluded my speech with a word-for-word translation of the blessing of *Modim* from the daily prayers, a blessing that really came alive for me as a result of this experience. Every word remains so personal to me:

---

6 *Toras Menachem Sefer Hama'amim* 5711–12, p. 110.

We are thankful to You, our G-d, forever and ever. You are the
strength of our life and the shield that saves us in every gener-
ation. We will give thanks to You and tell Your praises: for our
lives, which are in Your hands; our souls, which are kept securely
by You; and for the miracles that You perform for us every day;
and for Your wonders and goodness that are always with us,
evening, morning, and afternoon. You are merciful, and Your
kindness never stops, and we always put our hopes in You.

Finally, taking a fruit I had not yet eaten that season, I recited the blessing of *Shehecheyanu*, thanking G-d for having "given us life, sustained us, and enabled us to reach this special time," with careful emphasis on every single incredibly relevant word.

Chaya spoke as well. She began by calling Nissi's siblings up on stage, and then asked the crowd to give them a standing ovation. She proceeded to read a letter in Nissi's voice, thanking them for their cheerful visits, pictures, and love. They deserved the special attention—they'd really been an integral part of it all. She ended with a heartfelt thanks to our many friends, family members, and community who helped in so many ways. The evening concluded with Dr. Files's own very touching remarks, reminiscing about his first meeting with Nissi and the remarkable journey we'd been through.

We had invited the whole CICU staff to our celebration, despite knowing that they'd be too busy to come. Dr. McMullan sent his apologies that morning, as he was called in for an emergency surgery. But, to our surprise, Dr. Musa showed up, and gave Chaya a very warm embrace. When we later thanked her for making the time to come, she responded in an e-mail, "I couldn't miss it. The Divine intervention in his case was obvious."

After the beautiful event, our hearts still singing with the feelings of happiness and gratitude, we hopped into the van to drive my father to the airport. His flight back to Pittsburgh was scheduled for that evening, and before he left the Pacific Northwest, I had a treat in store for him. Never one to miss the opportunity to show off the natural beauty of the area, we found a small, quiet beach in West Seattle to watch the sun set over Elliott Bay, with the spectacular Olympic Mountains as the backdrop.

We unloaded everyone from the car...and the children exploded into the sand and surf, clothes and all. They ran straight into the chilly water, prancing and yelling with sheer delight and reckless abandon. It seemed like they intuitively, viscerally recognized that we'd broken through the constraints of the past six months. We felt the pressures of our new life melt in their pure joy, under the glow of a magical golden sunset.

But still, considering all the major events that were now in our rear-view mirror, I was desperate for a vacation. We attempted a hike out in the mountains, but between the hassle of schlepping Nissi's equipment and the general exhaustion, it wasn't proving to be the recharge such experiences usually accomplished for us. So I booked a rental house on the water near Gig Harbor, Washington; perhaps the getaway would prove to be the elixir we so badly needed.

On the way out, we stopped at an air show at McChord Air Force Base, which was thrilling for everyone except poor Nissi, who was obviously and rightfully terrified at the sounds of F-16 fighter jets screaming over his head. From there, we drove on to the quaint little house we had rented.

The house sat right over the water, and during low tide, the kids could play directly on the rock-strewn beach. Everyone was having a blast, until Shayna slipped and slit her leg on an oyster shell. I took one look at it and realized it needed stitches. I turned to Chaya and said, "Who will bring her to urgent care? You or me?" The two of us laughed wryly that with everything we'd been through, poor Shayna wasn't going to get very much sympathy! Shayna opted to have her mom take her to get it taken care of, and the brave kid got her knee sewn up. And from that point on during our vacation, I carried the ten-year-old on my shoulders any time we needed to walk anywhere beyond hopping distance.

THE HIGH HOLIDAY SEASON was now looming over us. With all the work and effort the holidays entail, let alone the college students we were supposed to serve, each day brought greater apprehension. I barely had the capability of breathing, let alone the energy to immerse myself in the intensity of the new year. I expressed this to Chaya, and she replied, "I think we need a Hawaii vacation." That sounded great to me! We enlisted my father-in-law, who agreed to come watch the older five children for a week after the conclusion of the holidays, and secured a timeshare in Maui—an island with a hospital—with the help of our good friends Dr. Craig Keebler and Dr. Carol Teitz.

The holidays were, as expected, intense. By the time the final holiday of the season, Simchas Torah, came along, I no longer felt capable of being the leader of the services. I was utterly exhausted. We left Seattle for Portland to spend a joyous but low-key Simchas Torah with our friends and colleagues on campus, the Bialos, and looked forward to our upcoming vacation.

Chapter 10

Aloha, Hawaii!

In planning for our rest and recovery in Maui, we did a bit of research to see what touristy experiences we'd be most interested in. Haleakalā National Park sounded fascinating: a drive up the ten-thousand-foot volcano to see what some people say is the best place in the word to watch sunrise and sunset. A little voice inside me said, "Wait! Isn't there something to be said about heart disease and high altitude?" A quick visit to the American Cardiac Association website told us all we need to know: no ascending altitudes higher than eight thousand feet, unless you had good left ventricular function. Well, considering Nissi has *no* left ventricle, Haleakalā was stricken from the list!

Although we'd been cleared for flight by Dr. Files, we were extremely apprehensive at takeoff. Chaya held Nissi, who slept soundly under a blanket, and the two of us didn't take our eyes off of him for the first hour of the flight. He slept wonderfully, and finally we started to let our guard down, and we ourselves fell asleep.

The rest of the flight was uneventful. After landing and collecting our luggage, we left the airport to get our rental car. When we walked outside of the terminal, getting our first taste of Hawaiian air and sun, the afternoon trade wind snapped at us vigorously. Nissi reacted as if panic-stricken—he arched his back and took desperate gulps of air. We immediately moved sideways to shelter him from the onslaught of air, which calmed him only slightly. We assumed he was having flashbacks or something of the sort from the oxygen blow-by during his hospital stays! That quickly set the tone for the vacation. Everything we did had to be planned around Nissi's fear of wind.

After settling into our apartment, we drove to a nearby Wal-Mart to stock up on food. As we headed to the checkout counter, we stole a look at a very happy Nissi—but his skin tone looked vaguely violet. Trying not to panic, we looked at each other and tried to assess the situation. On the one hand, he looked awful; on the other hand, he wasn't struggling in any way...What was going on? We paid for our food, somewhat comforted by the presence of a woman in front of us wearing medical scrubs, and rushed out the door, eager to put the pulse oximeter we had brought with us on him to gauge his actual oxygen sats. We rushed outside, and there in the bright Hawaii sun, we realized what the problem was—fluorescent lighting! The lighting in the store made him look terrible; in actuality, he was doing fine!

As the week progressed, we learned something fascinating about the recovery process. We had previously considered ourselves to be the type who enjoyed exciting activities and action. But when push came to shove, every activity that took effort—whether scuba diving or a lengthy drive—left us exhausted and feeling emotionally spent. On the other hand, simple afternoons just staring at the rhythmic waves, or trying to find sea turtles in the surf while watching the sunset, were experiences that began to provide the healing we were craving. We started to realize that we would never be the people we were before Nissi was born. The experience had really changed us within, and the things that had provided us with excitement beforehand were no longer interesting. Nissi's medical adventure left us with no appetite for any other adventure.

Late that week, after spending a few hours on a secluded beach just breathing in the fresh air, Chaya said to me, "You know, the sun and the water really make me happy." I took those words to heart and promised myself that if the time ever came to leave Seattle, we would head to a city with lots of sun and a seashore. In fact, about eight months after this vacation, we would be resettled in North Miami Beach, Florida.

IN THE MEANTIME, my military career was calling. As a somewhat new chaplain in the US Air Force Reserve, I still needed to take a six-week course at Maxwell Air Force Base in Alabama, the Basic Chaplaincy

Course. It had been pushed off because Nissi was in the hospital, but now that things had calmed down, I was told by my superiors to take the January course. The timing worked out, as it was winter break and Chaya could take the kids to her parents' home in Cincinnati for part of the time I would be in training.

Being away from the family is never fun, but add the stress of a complex medical child…and it made for a jumpy dad, to say the least. A few days after the family arrived in Cincinnati, Chaya reported that Nissi had been awake for most of the night with a croup-like cough. We tried to wait it out a day, but when I heard the cough over the phone, I told her to go to the doctor immediately.

She drove to the nearest urgent care. They didn't even finish listening to her report of his broader diagnoses before sending her right out the door to the ER at Cincinnati Children's Hospital. In the ER, they hooked him up to a pulse oximeter to check his sats. Upon seeing a reading in the 70s, the doctors just about rushed to intubate him. Chaya urgently held them up. "Stop! His base level is in the lower 80s! He's not doing that badly!"

They looked at her incredulously. "Are you sure?" They informed her that he'd be admitted to the CICU that night. They ran a battery of tests and confirmed that despite getting a vaccine to prevent it, Nissi had caught RSV (respiratory syncytial virus), a respiratory virus we knew was potentially lethal for high-risk children.

When Chaya called me with that information, I panicked. There is nothing like a parent's fear when their child is in an ICU half a country away.

The timing was remarkable; this happened on Wednesday, and our class would be given off Thursday in preparation for a field training over the weekend. We were told that the furthest we were allowed to go from the base was eight hours. I consulted Google maps—Cincinnati was eight hours, eight minutes away! I breathlessly informed my commander that I was heading to Cincinnati. "As long as you're back by 10:00 p.m. tomorrow," she told me.

I drove like a madman through Alabama, Tennessee, and Kentucky with every nightmare scenario playing out in my head. I tried desperately to listen to and internalize the positive messages of the Jewish music playing on the car stereo. At around midnight, I pulled up at Cincinnati Children's Hospital, and Chaya greeted me happily at the entrance of the hospital, telling me everything was stable.

We headed to Nissi's room, where we met the cardiologist, who greeted us cheerily. "I'm underwhelmed!" she laughed. "For a kid with his history to get RSV, he's doing extremely well. I could even let him go right now, but once he's here, we might as well keep him for observation overnight." Once again, his situation toyed with our emotions—swinging them from abject fear and dread to exhausted relief.

We slept overnight at the hospital, and in the morning, I stopped at my parents-in-law's house for a few hours, enjoying the brief chance to see the rest of the children before heading back to Alabama—a calmer and happier dad, and thankful to G-d yet again for His continuous miracles.

I was still in chaplaincy training for the most momentous first birthday any of us could imagine, and that meant that we could not celebrate quite the way we would have liked to, but we made do with a small FaceTime party. There was certainly a little feeling that this was a bit anticlimactic. After all, if every child's first birthday is worth celebrating, certainly this one's was, but at least we'd be able to celebrate in the future.

In any case, Nissi's birthday actually brought out complex feelings within us, a combination of absolute joy and vindication, along with a touch of sadness and pain at the memories of his traumatic birth. Perhaps nothing can express this better than what Chaya and I wrote on Facebook in honor and reflection of birthday number one.

Chaya wrote:

> *It's Nissi's birthday. His first. One we were told countless times—drilled into our hearts so we couldn't forget—that we wouldn't celebrate. Yet here I sit, holding a breathing, smiling, warm, and happy baby. His heart may be broken and patched, but it's beating strong. His heart and being have tightened our family bond, making us all love deeper and stronger. He has brought us a raw joy, a happiness that spreads from his little smile across the room. I feel so blessed and grateful for this gift of life, the gift of him, and the gift he's given our family.*

But today is a touch traumatic. It makes me sad and angry. His birth was not one of joy, of unwrapped expectations and possibilities. It was full of doom, of death about to happen. It was a tunnel of darkness. It was full of menacing people trying to steal our baby before his first breath was taken. Labels, assumptions, doomed expectations, and pain.

It's been a fight. A fight led by Nissi, joined by thousands of people worldwide who added his name to their Tehillim list, followed us on Facebook, added a mitzvah. It was fought by his parents, siblings, family, and doctors. People who didn't give up, give in to statistics, predictions, or dark doom.

It's been a journey of light, hope, love, and strength. It's been one that is fought anew each day. It's a battle of selflessness and patience, of mind control and heart expansion.

It's my new life—I'm a heart mom. I'm Nissi's mom.

As for me, well, I wrote something too...but not quite as beautiful. My Facebook post read:

Since my amazing wife expressed our sentiments on the occasion of Nissi's first birthday so beautifully, I've been relegated to sheer sarcasm.

> *Dear Dr. X,*
>
> *Thanks so much for your magnanimous offer and active assistance to help us bury our baby a tad early. We don't really regret to inform you that we waived his "right to die"; it was just that we don't really consider much the first word in the term "mercy killing." On a side note, considering that your predictions of a four-hour lifetime were, thank G-d, off by an order of magnitude, have you thought about trading in your doctor's coat for political prognostication? Just a thought I had. But seriously, I want to thank you for being a real-life example of "man plans, G-d laughs." I'd like to hope you're celebrating*

this occasion as much as we are; it's really beautiful to learn these life lessons in such a manner. Life really is the ultimate classroom, isn't it? Well, once we're using academic terms, I guess we might say Nissi flunked out of your hospice course, and isn't looking to go back there. #sorrynotsorry

And one last word from Nissi: "Giggle..."

Chapter 11

The Move to Miami

Themr rest of Basic Chaplaincy School went without incident, and I gratefully flew back to Seattle at the end of February. We had a lot to look forward to, even if it was not quite clear what was next for us and our family.

We had spent twelve and a half years in Seattle, doing whatever we could for every Jewish student we met. But now, considering our new responsibilities taking care of a medically complex and immunocompromised child along with the rest of our children, we realized we would never be able to give the incoming students the time and energy we had given them in the past. Those Shabbos dinners and conversations lasting past 2:00 a.m., the open home at all times, the nightly classes and discussions, would simply no longer be possible within the constraints of our new reality. It was time for someone else to take over this responsibility, while we would make sure to find a new rabbinic role within the family limitations we now had.

THE IDEA OF MIAMI came up in a conversation with my sister Nechama, who told me that she'd heard great things about the community in North Miami Beach. As things go, this conversation happened the day after I went to the Rebbe's gravesite and pleaded, "If it's time for us to move elsewhere, please give us the blessing of clarity: when and where." We quietly began researching the possibilities in Miami and were very happy with the results: a strong Chabad school, a vibrant Chassidic community in North Miami Beach, and a massive Jewish community in the general area with many job opportunities. We would eventually even get the chance to see it for ourselves, when Chaya's sister Esther announced her engagement that winter to a young man from North Miami Beach.

Miami looked better with every phone call we made, and it was soon obvious that we had been granted the blessing of clarity that we had requested at the Rebbe's gravesite. After celebrating Esther and Mendel's wedding, and sneaking in a few job interviews without the kids knowing it, things were looking up. We stayed an extra week in Miami to soak up the rays, courtesy of a vacation rental arranged by the wonderful people at Chai Lifeline. It was clear to us that the time had come to head south—from one corner of the United States to the other.

PASSOVER, which we spent with my parents in Pittsburgh, came and went. Soon after coming back to Seattle, Dr. Files sadly informed us that the heart regurgitation brought upon by the cardiac arrest was getting steadily worse. "I'm really sorry to tell you this, but Nissi needs to get his valve replaced."

Chaya was hesitant about the plan set forth by Dr. McMullan: to swap out his damaged common valve with a steel replacement valve. He was confident about the surgery, but told us that Nissi would be on Coumadin—the heaviest blood thinner that exists—for the rest of his life in order to avoid blood clotting around the artificial valve. Coumadin is also notoriously finicky; in order to ensure that the blood thinning levels are correct, he'd have to have his blood taken and sent to labs every two weeks.

Chaya was not happy about any of that. "We've already had one cardiac arrest due to a clot, and I'm not interested in going there again. Is there any chance at all we can repair the valve instead of replacing it?" Dr. McMullan wasn't particularly encouraging about that idea. "His valve is too damaged to repair, but maybe we can try."

Chaya's intuition pushed her to reach out to YL Hearts, a Jewish cardiac disease referral and support organization. The director of the organization, the indefatigable Mrs. Chaya Waks, agreed with her fears, and instructed her to reach out to Dr. Pedro del Nido, a famed surgeon at Boston Children's Hospital, who has particular expertise in heterotaxy children and valve repair. Dr. del Nido reviewed Nissi's scans and reported back, "Yeah, I'm sure we can repair that!" After getting confirmation from Dr. Files that Nissi would be okay until then, we booked a date for surgery in Boston toward the beginning of September.

In the meantime, the move to Miami was quickly coming upon us. While packing Nissi's supplies, going through the various and sundry papers, reports, and instructions from all his hospital stays, surgeries, and procedures, I came across a green piece of paper—the POLST form that had been forced upon us by the University Hospital NICU staff! Feeling particularly cheeky that day, I took Nissi in his stroller, and we went to say goodbye to the hospital that had given Nissi no hope for life. Chaya wanted no part of this adventure; for her, even driving past the hospital building was enough to bring on a bout of PTSD.

Upon visiting the labor and delivery ward, we had an intense conversation with the nurse who had taken care of us for the bulk of those four days. She was extremely gratified to see how well Nissi was doing. We also had the unfortunate occasion to have a conversation with one of the L&D doctors, who cavalierly dismissed everything we'd been through. ("Oh, we see kids like that all the time.") And from there, we went back to the NICU. Mae, the charge nurse who had given us the POLST, was—perhaps fortunately—not at work that day, so we left the POLST in an envelope with her name on it, and the message: "Keep fighting for babies' lives!" I felt deeply relieved—and emotionally spent—to walk out of the University Hospital building for the final time.

SHORTLY BEFORE OUR MOVE, I participated in making a minyan, a quorum of ten Jewish men, for the funeral of an unknown Jew. The section of the cemetery containing the final resting place of little children caught my eye and tugged at my heart. I uttered a prayer of deep thanks to G-d that my son was not there.

After the service and burial, I walked from the fresh gravesite together with the rest of the minyan. One of the other men present struck up conversation with me. He asked my name, and my response made him look at me with a funny expression. "Tell me," he asked gently. "Did you have a baby born a little while ago with severe medical problems?"

"Yes," I responded.

"Is it okay if I ask you how he's doing?"

"Sure! He's doing great. Why do you ask?"

"Because I am the head of the Seattle *chevrah kaddisha*. We were waiting for your call that day…"

I laughed exultantly. "And with G-d's help, you're never going to get it!"

THE MOVE TO MIAMI went without complications. I drove a truck with our possessions across the country, while Chaya and the four youngest children flew from Seattle, all of us arriving at our new home on the same day. Shayna flew from camp in California with several of her new classmates shortly after, and finally Yehuda arrived later from camp in New York. Providentially, we soon learned that just down the block lived an Orthodox Jewish nurse practitioner who worked in the Pediatric ICU at Miami's Nicklaus Children's Hospital. Jenny would be our go-to for any medical questions or advice during our first two years in Miami, until both of us moved houses.

Mrs. Waks of YL Hearts gave us strict instructions regarding our search for a new cardiologist: "Go to Dr. Anthony Rossi, at Nicklaus Children's Hospital." We took her suggestion seriously, especially considering the fact that there were several pediatric heart centers in the area. As soon as we got to Miami, we called his office. But his secretary shut things down quickly, saying, "Dr. Rossi is the director of the program, and he no longer accepts patients. But if you'd like, you can send your files to our office, and we'll see what he says." Sensing a possible breakthrough, we sent the files over e-mail. A short half hour later, the secretary called back with great news. "Dr. Rossi would like to know when you can come in for an appointment."

A short few days later, Dr. Rossi walked into the exam room and took his first look at Nissi. Nissi greeted him with a gigantic smile, and the genial Dr. Rossi began gushing, "Look at you! Aren't you so cute!"

To our surprise, instead of moving over to a medical conversation, he just continued to fawn over the gurgling baby. "He looks *so* good! I can't believe it!" Eventually, I interrupted him. "Dr. Rossi, I know he's doing well, but what in particular is so remarkable to you?" Dr. Rossi looked at me earnestly and said, "Listen. Firstly, as the head of the department,

I only really deal with very, very sick children. Sadly, it's rare that I get to meet a baby who looks so good. Secondly, I read through his files. He has an extensive medical history, as you obviously know. But there's no connection between the history that I read and the child I see here."

"What do you mean?" I persisted.

In his response, Dr. Rossi didn't mince words. "A child with *that* history, who has surprisingly survived all that he did, should be a shell of a human being—no eye contact, little response to voice stimuli, curled up in a ball. And—look at him! Look at that smile!" Turning back to Nissi, he launched back into full grandpa mode: "You are *so cute!*"

Eventually, we got back to the subject at hand: the plan. Dr. Rossi sadly agreed with Dr. Files that the valve replacement would need to be done sooner rather than later. I was hoping that we'd be able to do the surgery in Miami so as not to cause more chaos to the family—the cross-country move had already been disruptive enough.

He agreed to ask his surgical team to review the case. A few days later, he told us their thoughts: "Our surgical team is excellent, but they think the damage to the valve is pretty extensive. They can try to fix it, but they don't think they'll be able to. We really only have one shot at it, and if it doesn't work, we're going to have to go with the steel valve mid-surgery." Considering that hesitation in comparison with Dr. del Nido's complete confidence, we elected to bring him to Boston. Surgery would take place a few weeks before Rosh Hashanah, the Jewish New Year.

Chapter 12

A Hurricane Atop a Heart Surgery

There's always an adjustment period to be expected when making a major move, but we had little time to dwell on that. We'd have a scarce few weeks to furnish our new house and get settled for the school year, where I'd be teaching eighth and ninth grades. With the new job, I apprehensively broached the upcoming surgery with my new principal, who was understandably not thrilled at me taking off a few days at the beginning of the school year, so I opted to keep my participation in the surgery as short as possible.

Boston Children's medical team asked us to come a week before surgery for pre-op, followed by a catheterization on Thursday to measure out Nissi's current blood flows and pressures in order to get the best sense of the situation. The actual procedure, in which Dr. del Nido would shorten and tighten the miniscule anchors of the valve flaps, was planned for the following Monday. Given that, the plan was for Chaya and Nissi to travel to Boston first, and for me to join them there on the Sunday before surgery. As we set on this plan, a storm—literally—began brewing on the horizon: Hurricane Irma.

Irma was heading straight for South Florida, with Miami directly in her sights. My mother-in-law flew to Miami to lend us a hand just before Chaya and Nissi left for Boston, and we followed the weather reports religiously as Irma crept closer. Veteran Floridians laughed away the fearmongering, the hoarding, and the frenetic preparations, but I was far more concerned about something else: flight cancellations.

As the date for the surgery converged over the expected landfall of the hurricane, I realized that the family was going to need to take refuge someplace far enough away from the storm that I would still be able to fly to Boston. A day before Irma's outer bands reached Florida, Wednesday afternoon, we decided to make a run for it and head for my brother Sholom's house in Atlanta.

My brain was truly in a tizzy—I could barely think. Between the new teaching job, the hurricane, the surgery, and my wife (a woman I like to refer to as "my better three-quarters") away, I simply couldn't think straight. I usually can put things in some semblance of order with her, but now everything was converging on me. I felt incredibly overwhelmed. Thankfully, my mother-in-law was able to focus me a bit. My brother-in-law Motti, who was studying in a local rabbinical school for the year, helped the kids take down the trampoline and secure the garbage cans, and I packed my precious book collection in watertight crates. We threw some clothes and snacks into the car and headed out onto the highway in an attempt to get to Atlanta.

This close to the storm's expected hit, gas stations had been emptied of all their fuel, and we were hard pressed to find gas along the way. Luckily, when driving to pick up a sister-in-law who was studying in high school in Coral Springs, we happened upon a gas station that had just refilled. After topping off the fuel tank, we headed onto the highway...which was stacked with traffic beyond belief. An eight-hour drive turned into twenty-two, including a stop at Chabad at University of Florida, in Gainesville. Rabbi Goldman graciously opened his kosher deli for us, feeding our very hungry family at no cost. I can't really tell you how, but somehow, we survived that trip with everyone's sanity intact, totally devoid of the typical bickering notorious of car trips.

The worst moment on the trip was a bathroom stop on the side of the highway. When we got back in the car, Levi yelped in pain. Red ants had made their way into the car and were biting him! I jumped into the back of the minivan and killed the bugs with my fingers, getting bitten a few times myself in the process.

When we finally, thankfully, arrived in Atlanta, I jumped on the very first flight available to Boston to join Chaya. Things were very quiet in Boston; while we were fighting our agonizing way through traffic, Chaya was told they'd canceled the cardiac catheterization that had been planned. One less medical procedure under anesthesia sounded great, so we didn't make a big deal about it.

All things considered, particularly with the news of Hurricane Irma on everyone's minds and blaring off of every TV, Chaya had been the recipient of triple doses of sympathy from anyone she met. Conversations went something like this:

"What are you in town for?"

"My son's open-heart surgery."

"Awww...Where's your husband?"

"Well, we just moved, so he couldn't take off extra work."

"Just moved?! Oh boy...you poor thing. Where did you move to?"

"Miami..."

"?!?!!!"

I WAS OVERJOYED to be reunited with her, and doubly thrilled to put the chaos of our trip behind me. In nervous anticipation of surgery, we toured the USS Constitution and other Boston historic sites. As we took Nissi in and out of the car seat, we began to notice that despite the car's air conditioning and the comfortable autumn weather, his shirt was drenched in sweat, and he was pretty sleepy. We didn't think much of it...until Monday.

We were brought into the pre-op room first thing Monday morning. Nissi was in a particularly cheerful mood, especially when one of the nurses brought over a Little Tikes car for him to sit in. This being his first time in a toy like that, he sat there with a cherubic grin that lit up the room. The hustle and bustle of children heading out to various and sundry surgeries made no difference to him—he was loving it!

The nurses began the anesthesia drip, and Dr. del Nido came by to introduce himself. After the perfunctory hellos, he told us the surgical plan, and then added something quite shocking: "You probably noticed that we canceled the cardiac catheterization on Thursday. Well, that's because your son's heart is regurgitating over 50 percent. That means that over 50 percent of the blood his heart should be pumping to his body is splashing around his heart without getting sent to the rest of the body. As a result, his heart is working well over twice as hard as it should. In fact, he actually should be in heart failure." He looked over at Nissi and pointed to his glowing smile. "We have no idea how he looks like that, but he shouldn't. We were afraid that if we did the cardiac catheterization, it could very well kill him. That's why we canceled it. It also means that it is absolutely urgent that we do this surgery now, but I'm confident he'll do well."

We were quite stunned by that pronouncement, to say the least! Putting two and two together, we realized that the sweat-drenched shirt on the sleepy child had actually been a sign of tremendous danger, signs of his heart working way too hard to support the basic function of a virtually immobile little boy. As the reality of how close he had come to death yet again dawned on us, we looked at our happy little toddler with even greater appreciation of G-d's continuous miracles.

Dr. del Nido wandered backstage to continue his pre-op prep, but before he did, we once again requested he ask the surgical team to take on positive resolutions for Nissi's sake, which he agreed to do happily. Soon, the entire pre-op ward had emptied out, with just us, Nissi, and his nurse remaining. Surprised, the nurse pointed out that the drugs should have knocked him out already, but he was still happily playing and babbling. A full half hour passed, as the nurse added more and more narcotics, until finally his eyelids started drooping. We kissed him softly on the head, watched him as the nurse wheeled him away, and then proceeded to take turns pacing the length of the waiting room while saying *Tehillim* in nervous anticipation.

Several hours later, Dr. del Nido came back with the news of a successful repair. "Everything went extremely well. His heart looks better than it ever has," he stated. We asked about the original TAPVC repair, which we knew could be very tricky. "Oh, that looks great," he said. And after a bit of a pause he said, "You know, your son's heart anatomy is completely messed up...but its *function* is truly phenomenal." Only a surgeon could give a compliment like that!

Recovery from surgery was fairly routine, with the routine scares. As the heart did its best to recover, it would occasionally launch into stratospheric arrhythmias—several times topping well over two hundred beats per minute instead of the normal 70–110 beats per minute, due to severe SVTs, the "salsa" rhythms we had experienced after previous surgeries. Boston's team kept him in the CICU while they worked to get that under control, and it eventually settled down.

Surprisingly, the cardiologist appointed over his care was Dr. Snow—the same doctor who had written "surgery is futile" in response to our request for a second opinion prenatally. That made me uncomfortable, to say the least. I kept expecting an apology of some sort, or perhaps a recognition that surgery had not been "futile," but none was forthcoming. Every conversation kept getting more and more stressful; his cold and perfunctory attitude rubbed us the wrong way, in addition to his inability to own up to the prenatal mistake he'd made. "It was obviously heterotaxy. Those prenatal scans showed classic signs of the syndrome," he told us one day, oblivious to our upset reactions. While he remained on the team—against our will—for the duration of our stay, we insisted on getting a different cardiologist when we would next come to Boston, for the Fontan procedure.

Soon after Nissi woke up from surgery, we thought it was time to get him eating again, and the nurse provided us with a bottle of chocolate PediaSure to start things off. He had been making strides in his eating, even eating pretzels in the days leading up to surgery, and we wanted to maintain the positive movement. Well, he eagerly drank the bottle, but his stomach just as eagerly sent it right back up from whence it came with a torrential flow. We were later told that sometimes heart surgery inexplicably creates feeding aversion, and that's what had happened here. All of our hard work trying to get him to eat during the past year went right out the window. It would be over three years until the next time he ate a pretzel. Hey, in Nissi's world, it seems like eating is overrated anyway!

IN THE MEANTIME, I needed to get back to the rest of my children, whom I had last left in Atlanta at my brother Sholom's house, under the watch of my mother-in-law. After trouncing the Florida peninsula, Hurricane Irma had headed straight up to Atlanta, where its heavy rains and strong winds knocked the power out there as well. Providentially, Shayna fell awkwardly off a hoverboard, and my mother-in-law took her to the emergency room to get her rapidly swelling arm assessed. She was diagnosed with a hairline fracture, and had a cast placed on it. I say providentially, because while they were at the hospital, a tree fell over the street, blocking access to the cul-de-sac in which my brother Sholom's house stood. From that point until the tree was removed, my van was used to get supplies for the two families.

A few days after surgery, I flew back to Atlanta and took the reins back from my incredible mother-in-law, who happily returned home to Cincinnati. The return ride to Miami was done in a brief eight hours, surrounded by hordes of electrical repair trucks. The drive down the I-75 was surreal, with evidence of the violence of the storm scattered on both sides of the highway: huge trees splintered, billboards shredded, and road signs mangled.

Electricity had been knocked out in North Miami Beach for several days by the time I arrived back home, and nightmarish scenes of cockroaches amid spoiled food flooding my house flitted through my imagination throughout the drive. Fortunately, there was little damage to the house, and no sign of cockroaches, but with the lack of air conditioning, the house was sweltering and virtually unlivable. A family offered to host us until the electricity came back on, and we gladly took them up on the offer. Thankfully, we got our power back before Rosh Hashanah; others in the neighborhood weren't so lucky. The community banded together in a truly beautiful way, despite the fact that Rosh Hashanah was quickly approaching, providing free food and assistance to anyone who needed it.

My parents flew down to Miami to help us for the holidays. Chaya would spend Rosh Hashanah in the hospital with Nissi, as he was on the mend but not quite ready for discharge. Chaya's brother Yeshaya came to Boston and split his time between visiting her in the hospital and getting to know his future in-laws.

Rosh Hashanah itself was surreal for Chaya, not exactly spiritual in the traditional or typical manner, as her prayers were interrupted by alarms, doctors, and the general work of tending to Nissi's needs. But there was something absolutely raw about the reflections and prayers about life and health while battling for those very blessings. The beauty and simplicity of the words of Rosh Hashanah's devotional prayers, said while watching the steady movement of her toddler's just-recently-opened chest, made the tears flow freely. The gratitude, the hopes, the fervent wishes—they all wrapped themselves together into a mother's earnest prayers for a *shanah tovah* in the truest sense.

On the day following Rosh Hashanah, Boston Children's discharged Nissi, repaired heart and all, to come back home.

Chapter 13

Therapy—
Physical and Spiritual

T he month of Tishrei and its holidays ended off on the enervated yet exuberant notes of Simchas Torah. We began to settle into a routine: Chaya took over as Nissi's full-time caretaker, while I worked and tried to give support and guidance whenever I had breaks in my school day.

Prior to leaving Seattle, we had an MRI to assess Nissi's brain. I had been very loath to agree to that MRI. My attitude was that whatever damage was there, was there; we weren't going to change our attitude toward him as a person, and we didn't want the medical staff to look at him as lesser than a regular human being. As it was, he was evidently "with it"—social, happy, aware, and it seemed like he had full range of movement in all of his limbs, even if he didn't quite sit up or crawl yet. We expected delays; after all, his first few months of life were anything but typical. But despite my hesitation, the neurologist insisted on it, and the MRI was done around the same time a catheterization was done so we could avoid putting him under anesthesia any more than absolutely necessary.

The results showed there was some minimal but clear scarring in the mobility area of his brain, which added cerebral palsy to his already long list of diagnoses. We both had a hard time swallowing that new diagnosis, maybe because of the fear of the permanence of brain damage, perhaps because of the harshness to which we associated that particular term. Or maybe it was because we had been so sure that his delays would just play catch-up with a little therapy, as they had with Yehuda, or simply because we were overwhelmed by the idea of another major medical area to navigate. Our denial and fear were obvious at our follow-up visit, but the neurologist patiently explained to us that the official diagnosis of cerebral palsy would assist to get Nissi more services and help rather than less. But she agreed that, as parents, we should not allow it to dictate our expectations in any way. We sincerely appreciated her thoughtfulness and encouragement.

WHEN THINGS SETTLED DOWN in Miami, we began a plethora of therapies, beginning with physical and occupational therapies (PT and OT), along with language, feeding, and water therapies. Later we added Feldenkrais therapy, and as of this writing we have been accepted into a horse therapy program that will start sometime in the next school year. Juggling schedules has always been a royal hassle—between all the above plus his many appointments with doctors spanning a spectrum of specialties, it is an ongoing battle to ensure his therapies stay consistent.

Nissi is a therapist's dream child—or, at least, he was. There's a lot to work on, but he has been gifted with an unbelievably sunny disposition and seems almost impervious to pain. His social sensitivity is off the charts; even as a baby, he would make eye contact with passersby and smile at them until he got a reaction. Cashiers, neighbors, and therapists alike seem to be totally taken by him. We joke that because he only has half a heart, he needs to steal everyone else's to make up for it.

I only say "was" a dream child, because now his sense of humor is such that he's become a real *ipcha mistabranik*—the kind of kid who'll do the exact opposite of what you tell him to do, and his golden giggle just echoes across the room, causing anyone within earshot to start laughing, whether or not they know what's going on. And with that laugh...it's pretty hard to get serious with him. What are you going to bribe or threaten him with? With the feeding pump still supplying his nutrition, he doesn't eat much (he even says matter-of-factly, "I don't need to eat"). Nowadays, it takes a lot of patience and discipline to work with him. Still, he works hard at everything and celebrates every hard-earned success with a smile from ear to ear and pure, sweet laughter.

Nissi's physical abilities—mobility and fine motor skills—have developed in agonizingly slow motion. Throughout all this time, he has never plateaued, but every simple movement, such as grasping things with his hands, sitting up himself, holding his trunk straight and tall, is a hard-won accomplishment, the result of months of tireless effort. He never complains, but as he's gotten older, despite it all, we find ourselves racked by conflicting feelings: the sadness of what he can't do intermingling with the joy of how much he has persevered. But Nissi seems to ignore his limitations, or, at least, he takes them in stride. He somehow has the mature understanding that we all should have: life, with all its flaws, is truly a gift.

The optimal therapy schedule that we aim for is two hours a day, four days a week, but getting there has proven to be a fight, as we have to shift our schedules to mesh with that of the different therapists. Eventually, after quite a bit of frustration, we found a team that has more than just the skill to help Nissi; they have the passion and concern. We knew we'd found the right physical therapist the very first time we met Vanessa: she was visibly horrified at hearing Nissi's birth story. And indeed, she has become the advocate we needed for so long, making sure to give Nissi every advantage in his quest to start walking.

There have been therapy days that have been incredible and days that are draining. The small, unexpected accomplishments, the words of encouragement from the therapists—those make the schlep all over town and the hard work feel worth it. But there are also days when Chaya feels completely frustrated, such as when exercises at home aren't accomplished because of the drama of regular life, or when a neighborhood kid who was once at the same developmental stage as Nissi has surpassed him by leaps and bounds, or when the effort of sifting through vast amounts of programs to find the right therapist and therapies for Nissi's level of complexity is just too overwhelming.

The physical exhaustion of carrying him as he grows bigger, coupled with the emotional baggage of caring for a complex child, can overwhelm her. A mother always wants to give her child everything possible to succeed in life, and with a special-needs child, there is no end to what needs to be done, and that can drive even the strongest mom to tears.

On days like that, I encourage her to just muddle through and try to cut herself some slack by focusing on the big picture: how much progress he has made despite it all, and how far we've come. Besides whatever encouragement I can offer, Nissi can accomplish even more. A hug, a smile, and his sincere and charming "Mommy, thank you! You're the best!" is usually enough to get us all back on track.

Speech has come with time, and with it a spunky, cheeky sense of humor. Even when he was very little, he had a knack for delivering comedic punchlines with perfect timing. For example, at a Friday night Shabbos table, as we were all eating Chaya's delicious chicken soup, three-year-old Nissi was given a single soup crouton, upon which he promptly gagged. I shoved his high chair away from the table as he began to vomit violently. When things calmed down a bit, and he'd barely caught his breath, he looked up and said (quoting a children's video), "Nom, nom, nom—delicious!"

Add to that humor an unmatched enthusiasm: when given an opportunity that he's excited about, he'll respond with a drawn-out, exaggerated, "Yaaaaaaaaay!"

As mentioned, PT and OT have made much slower progress than speech, so OT ordered him a special stroller, an adjustable high chair and, most importantly, a "gait trainer." The gait trainer is a wheelchair-like contraption that allows him to stand and mimic the motion of walking, thereby giving him the ability to propel himself around the house. He only really figured out how to use it consistently around his fourth birthday.

But with the stroller, which gave him much better trunk support than the average stroller, I started bringing him to synagogue. Or, more accurately, he started insisting I bring him to synagogue. And despite the difficulty of it, I am always happy to. First, the connection to holiness is definitely something we want to instill and foster in all our children, and Nissi is no different. But secondly, every mitzvah and G-dly connection means that much more when you know that every moment of life is all a gift from Above.

Nissi quickly became the synagogue mascot; his unabashed "amen!" in response to the cantor echoes across the sanctuary. As he began to talk more, I would work to hush him up so as not to disturb the other worshippers. And invariably a friend would come over to me and say, "Hey; G-d cares more about his babbling than your prayers. So leave him alone!"

Nissi will stand leaning against the backrest of the pew with his ear-to-ear smile, making eye contact with everyone in the synagogue, melting the hearts of all present. And when the Torah is taken out of the ark to be read, he virtually jumps out of his seat to kiss it. One respected member of the community, a family practitioner, told me one week: "You have no idea—I had a miserable week this week. I really tried to put it aside for Shabbos, but it was really hard. And then when I saw Nissi kiss the Torah? With that smile?! All my problems disappeared!" Nissi really has become an integral part of the community, and this despite the fact that most people don't even know most of his story. They just see a boy who doesn't stop smiling at the world.

Nissi's unbelievable joy is an antidote to any pain—both his own, as well as the sadness of anyone around him. The kid's default mode is pure, unadulterated joy. And on the rare occasion he gets upset, he snaps back almost immediately, with no trace of melancholy remaining. Here's a classic example: Once, soon after he received his G-tube, as we will soon recount, I picked him up, and the tube got stuck on the corner of a chair and yanked at his stomach, nearly pulling it out. Uncharacteristically, he began to cry, so we knew he was in real pain. Chaya held him close. He buried his head in Chaya's chest, crying for about fifteen seconds, and then picked his head up, gave it a little shake, and with the tears still wet on his face said, "Happy now!"

His siblings can no longer get upset with him around anymore; if they do, Nissi toddles over to them in his gait trainer, and, with an earnest face or a gigantic grin, says something like, "Menachi, be happy!" And who can resist that?! It is, to a large degree, his superpower.

AS HE MOVED PAST his second birthday, his feeding therapy was moving so agonizingly slowly, it could barely be described as moving. Eating through four single pieces of Bamba in a half hour weekly session would be considered successful. We realized that we needed a more long-term solution than the NG tube. Chaya had replaced it herself dozens of times, slipping the flexible tube, quick as a pro, down the nose of the screaming, squirming toddler—but it simply wasn't fair to him anymore. A G-tube would be a far more functional way of making sure he got fed, as the likelihood of it coming out was much slimmer than the NG Tube, which seemed to come out every other day. When we put in a request to the GI team, they readily agreed that it was an excellent idea, so another surgery was planned, but thankfully, this one was not emergent.

As the date of the surgery approached, I had a brainstorm—could we get a circumcision done at the same time? He'd not had a *bris milah* yet, because for him, any such procedure would need to be done under cardiac anesthesia. I contacted Rabbi Yochanan Klein, director of a medical assistance organization called Healing Hearts and a mohel himself, to discuss the possibility. He arranged with a Jewish urologist associated with Nicklaus Children's to have the bris done immediately following the G-tube placement, while Nissi would still be in the operating room.

Nissi was two and a half years old at this point. Unlike the typical eight-day-old infant, he was very much awake and part of the traditional pre-bris celebration, as neighborhood children came over to say *Shema* with him on the night before his surgery. Nissi very happily said *Shema* along with all them, knowing and enjoying that he was the center of everyone's attention.

We asked the rabbi of our local community, Rabbi Yossi Marlow, to be the sandek, the one honored with holding the child, for this very special bris. It was imperative to me that he and Rabbi Klein understand the power of the moment, so I sent them a very early draft of this book to help them understand what Nissi had been through.

The next morning found us joyously but nervously greeting the friends who had made the trek through traffic to join us for the bris in the surgical waiting lounge. We crowded around, talking quietly. I had brought some Torah material with me to study during the wait, but, needless to say, I couldn't concentrate.

The first part of the surgery, the G-tube placement, took far longer than usual. We later learned that this was because his anatomy is so confusing, so everything needed to be done virtually backward. His G-tube therefore sits on his right side, while anyone else with a G-tube has theirs on their left. In addition, the surgeon had to cut through all the scar tissue from his previous surgeries. Later, the surgeon also informed us that Nissi's diaphragm had been paralyzed as a result of the previous surgery, and his stomach had moved up into the vacancy and gotten stuck there. It had taken a significant amount of time and effort to stretch the stomach downward and tack it into place. Nothing was routine for this kid.

Eventually, Rabbi Marlow, Rabbi Klein, and I were suited up head to toe in surgical scrubs in preparation for this unique bris. We were called back by an intern, and Rabbi Marlow and Rabbi Klein entered the operating room, while I was told to stand in the doorway. As the sandek, Rabbi Marlow was instructed to put his hands below Nissi's head during the procedure, while Nissi slept blissfully under anesthesia. The urologist did most of the cutting, while Rabbi Klein recited the preparatory prayers, and then signaled for me to make the blessing thanking G-d for the commandment to "bring this child into the Covenant of Abraham." So surreal was the experience, I missed his first signal. But eventually I said it loudly and with feeling. At the end of the ceremony, we headed out to wish mazel tov to everyone and await the conclusion of the surgery.

We had a festive meal of bagels and lox for those hardy enough to have waited for us all those hours. It was small, intimate, and reverberating with feeling. I was shaking from the fatigue of the all-night learning the previous evening, as well as the emotion of the moment. To have reached this point, where Nissi was medically stable enough to officially join the Covenant of Abraham with a *bris milah*, was almost unbelievable. The congratulatory mazel tovs we received took on such depth. They expressed that we'd reached a new point in his journey: we could finally begin to celebrate his life milestones, and not just react and recover from medical crises.

It truly was a *bris milah* like no other—for a kid like no other.

Chapter 14

A Special Birthday

L ife had changed. We were, thankfully, no longer living on the edge. The miracles, too, were more subtle, evidenced in the finer details. He'd often wake up in the morning soaked in vomit from his reflux, yet all smiles. He somehow has never suffered from aspiration, despite being unable to completely roll over.

And then there is the fact that he has no spleen. In theory, without that organ, which functions to clean blood and support the immune system, he should get sick often. But he doesn't. Yet despite his stamina, we're always on guard. A cough or a sniffle mean nothing to a regular child, but to one this complex could be evidence of something very dangerous. We have an intercom in his room to hear him when he sleeps, and we jump at the slightest rustle. Most parents simply cannot understand the level of care and concern that we are tasked with, but we have formed unique friendships with other parents of medically complex children who understand our fight to keep him safe. One such dad has even appointed himself our "security guard" in our synagogue, brusquely shooing away anyone who gets near Nissi, while barking, "Don't touch him! Do you want him to get sick?!" The hypervigilance is both necessary and stressful. During the COVID-19 coronavirus breakout, we kept Nissi at home for months on end, only venturing out with him for the occasional walk around the block. But despite our caution, Chaya, and Nissi's two roommates, Levi and Menachi, came down with the virus in December 2020. Incredibly, Nissi didn't contract the bug at all.

The winter we moved to Miami, he had a mild bout of the flu and was hospitalized briefly for observation. It was then that we realized how lucky we had been in Seattle, with the hospital in such close proximity.

Depending on traffic, Nicklaus Children's can be as far as a forty-five-minute drive from us, so when he's hospitalized, it makes things a bit more difficult for us. But he plowed through the flu with a slight increase in his daily amoxicillin dose, and came home a few days later, none the worse for wear.

With the relatively calmer life, we began preparing for a very special date: Nissi's third birthday and the traditional first haircutting—his *upsherenish*.

This was not to be a typical third-birthday party. Rather, our goal was for everyone who came to get a sense of the magnitude of the milestone, even if they didn't know all the details of his story. It was crucial to us that the party expressed our thanks to G-d in an obvious manner. We wanted the setting itself, rather than endless speeches, to evoke the feelings.

For our ex-preemie Yehuda's *upsherenish*, also a very powerful event, we had prepared a little video, which included several clips from a TV show about preemies that we'd been featured on, mixed with home videos, showing his miraculous growth. We considered creating something like that but felt that a similar project for Nissi would be too labor intensive and expensive. Instead, we made a photo journal of the experience, courtesy of Shutterfly. Honestly, the process of picking the pictures was quite stressful. As we went through our hundreds of pictures from those early hospital stays, the feelings and emotions of those painful, intense days came flooding back. Eventually, we produced a photo book that depicted the general story in a broader way, in full color, and as a by-product, also provided us with elements of closure and catharsis.

Living in Florida's tropical weather, we decided to hold the festivities in our backyard. For the decor, we chose his favorite color, green, and accented it with silver and black. Balloons and charity boxes peppered the tables. We followed a similar theme to Nissi's *seudas hoda'ah*, when we'd decorated the tables with various quotes about miracles. This time we featured verses from Torah that expressed our appreciation to G-d for everything we'd been through, and hung them above or below large pictures of Nissi from various stages of his young but adventurous life, which were hanging on the white lattice wall of our Sukkah adjacent to our house. The quotes we chose were:

הודו לה׳ כי טוב כי לעולם חסדו—*Praise G-d for He is good; for His kindness is everlasting.*[1]

הפכת מספדי למחול לי פתחת שקי ותאזרני שמחה—*You turned my mourning into dancing; you opened my sackcloth and clothed me with joy.*[2]

לא אמות כי אחיה ואספר מעשי י–ה—*I shall not die, but I shall live and recount G-d's deeds.*[3]

קטונתי מכל החסדים ומכל האמת אשר עשית את עבדיך—*I have been humbled by all the acts of kindness and by all the truth that You have done for Your servant.*[4]

כי חילצת נפשי ממות את עיני מן דמעה את רגלי מדחי—*For You have delivered my soul from death, my eyes from tears, and my feet from stumbling.*[5]

One more poster featured Nissi's name in Hebrew and a list of several of his diagnoses and the major procedures he'd been through. It read:

Nesanel

- Complex congenital heart disease
- Heterotaxy syndrome
- Hospice care
- Four open-heart surgeries
- Two abdominal surgeries
- Cardiac arrest
- ECMO
- Multiple procedures and hospitalizations…

…I'm a miracle!

---

1   *Tehillim* 118:1.
2   Ibid. 30:12.
3   Ibid. 118:17.
4   Genesis 32:11.
5   *Tehillim* 116:8.

The day of the party arrived. Our yard quickly filled with laughter, smiles, and the occasional "wow" as people tried to grasp the magnitude of all the little birthday boy had been through. Looking through the pictures and then back at the cheeky smile before them, it was hard to imagine this was the same kid!

We had also contacted a local TV station and invited them to interview us for a feel-good story for their news broadcast. To our joy, the reporter they sent was a fellow Jew, Ian Margol. He gladly put on tefillin before he interviewed us, and he ended up playing an important role in the party.

The custom in the Chabad community is to honor someone from the priestly tribe, and then someone from Levite descent, for the first two snips of the little boy's hair. As we began the proceedings, the Levite we had honored with the second cut texted me frantically. He was stuck somewhere and was running late. We tried waiting for a little bit, but at some point, we just had to start without him. I called out to the crowd, "Do we happen to have a Levite here?"

Looking a bit confused, Ian, the reporter, raised his hand. "I am..." he said hesitantly.

Overjoyed, I handed him the scissors. "In that case, the honor is all yours!" He was visibly touched by the honor and the experience. And that evening, our little miracle boy's birthday party was featured on the nightly news.

After the party, we sat around the living room and watched the newsclip, surrounded by our loving extended family, our children, and Nissi. Our appreciation for reaching this milestone knew no bounds, and the bright future ahead filled us with deep gratitude.

Chapter 15

The Fontan

How many times had we heard, "The first year is the most dangerous for single-ventricle kids"? Nissi had scooted through that year by the skin of his teeth. And with so much in our rearview mirror, it was with a bit of apprehension that we set our sights on the next goal: the third and hopefully final heart repair, the Fontan procedure.

The goal of the Fontan is to make blood from the lower part of the body go directly to the lungs. This lets the blood pick up oxygen without having to pass through the heart. In this surgery, they would disconnect the Glenn setup, insert a new, large Gore-Tex tube, and this would be the final repair of his single ventricle defect.

I wasn't too eager to return to Boston. After all, Nicklaus Children's Hospital has an excellent staff with a world-class group of surgeons. But as good as they are, they had never dealt with Nissi's unique cardiac anatomy; Boston Children's surgeons had. Would it really make much of a difference? Perhaps it would be better for our family if Nissi stayed local, so we could care for him as a family? But Chaya's intuition felt strongly that Boston was the right place for the Fontan.

We went back and forth on these questions and eventually brought them to Dr. Rossi for his perspective. He was thoughtful, and then he said, "We have an excellent team here in Miami, but you really can't compare a team that has already been inside his heart to a team that has not. If this were my son, I would take him back to Boston."

With a caring, concerned response like that, the decision was made. Once again, we booked tickets and a room in Boston Children's Hospital, this time for July 2019. Most of our kids would be in camp, and once again, our parents would kindly step in and help out by watching the youngest ones.

In advance of this surgery, our feelings were much different from the previous ones. He was in such good shape and had so much strength that it was hard to think that he needed another surgery. His stamina itself was incredible—he seemed to have no limits as to how long he could stay up with a smile on his face. On late nights such as Purim, Simchas Torah, or Passover, he insisted on being part of the celebrations, all the way to the end. He always wanted to dance on my shoulders, and never seemed to tire out, despite the fact that most cardiac kids cannot expend much energy due to their hearts working so hard just to function. It was easy to forget, or not even notice, his illness. This was illustrated humorously when he was brought to Boston for surgery. Our children's entire school said *Tehillim* for him. But afterward, nine-year-old Levi commented, "Why did my teacher say he's sick? Nissi isn't 'sick'!" It was hard to consider putting him back in the hospital and having his poor chest opened up for the seventh time. At the same time, we knew it had to be done, and we hoped that his strength would stand him in good stead for an easy recovery.

Chaya went to Boston first, as usual. By this time, I'd been working for the Aleph Institute as their military personnel liaison, a dream job that pulled together my military life responsibilities with my rabbinic life responsibilities. My bosses at Aleph were very understanding, but I still didn't want to take off too much work. My mother met Chaya in Boston, and they were graciously hosted by her brother Yeshaya's new parents-in-law for the pre-op week, and I joined them on Sunday, the day before the surgery.

Things proceeded apace with check-in, a catheterization, and then a quiet weekend before the big day—first thing Monday morning. All the while, we were hearing exactly the words we wanted to hear from the usually skeptical doctors: "I don't want to sound Pollyannaish, but he really looks extraordinarily good!"

We met Dr. del Nido in the pre-op room, and once again he had something moving to say. "It was good that you came here to fix the valve. The Fontan is dependent on strong pulmonary flow, and Nissi's looks great as a result of that fix. Had they put in a steel valve, it would have made his lungs much weaker, and possibly not allowed him to be a candidate for the Fontan."

Yet another close call...I looked at Chaya with deep appreciation for her determined insistence on listening to her maternal instinct, guided as it was from Above.

Dr. del Nido again agreed to ask the team to take on positive resolutions in Nissi's merit, and with a promise of, "We'll take good care of him," they took Nissi to the operating room for his Fontan. Chaya and I found ourselves a quiet spot to say *Tehillim*, with deep thanks to G-d for the past, and devotional request for the future.

For the most part, surgery went well. Along with the Fontan setup, they also widened the opening of one of the pulmonary veins. They had also attempted to stitch his diaphragm down to resolve the paralysis, but the intense power of that muscle ripped the stitches out almost immediately, and the diaphragm went right back to whence it had come. It remains a note in his records until he eventually outgrows it. He came back to us, still asleep, for a calm, quiet day. When he finally woke up, they extubated him successfully, and we even got in a brief conversation:

Nissi: "Hi!"

Chaya: "Hi, Nissi! Are you tired?"

Nissi: "No."

And then he promptly fell back asleep.

The next time he woke up, he had all the excitement of a drunken sailor, babbling happily and somewhat insensibly for twelve hours, until he finally conked out again.

THE POSTOPERATIVE GAME WAS BACK ON—trying to get him off oxygen and watching little arrhythmias to make sure they didn't turn into something bigger. But his lungs were not healing quite as quickly as we would have liked. He also spiked a fever, which kept him in the ICU a few more days than expected. That turned out to be from an infection in the surgical site. At the time, we didn't realize how dangerous that could be, but the team remained extra cautious about it as they treated it with the heaviest antibiotics they could. I was getting very edgy, wondering why we couldn't fly him back to Miami, and if we had any problems we'd just bring him to Nicklaus Children's. In hindsight, I realize that I was jumping the gun, and thankfully, the team remained set on keeping him for a bit longer.

The Chabad rabbis in the Boston area had been feeding us this entire time, splitting up meals between themselves and delivering them to us. That Shabbos, as we made Kiddush and had our little meal in the darkened room next to a sleeping Nissi, we opened a thermos of soup provided to us by Mrs. Chanie Posner, formerly Chaya's fourth-grade teacher. The soup was still piping hot, and the delicious, fresh taste of the chicken soup revived us in a way that cannot really be described. It made for a very special Shabbos, a small return to sanity.

The day I was to fly back to Miami, they finally moved Nissi out of the CICU and onto the post-op floor. Chaya had been asking them all week to give her a single room so she could have some privacy, particularly for Shabbos, so it was very upsetting when we were moved into a double room. All of our stuff was packed into a small corner of the room, which barely fit the recliner. The nurse who brought us there was not helpful in the slightest, so we went up the chain of command and asked to be moved to a different room.

A few hours later, the nurse entered without a word to us or eye contact, and headed to our roommate's curtain. We were able to make out a bit of activity from behind the curtain on the other side of the room. It seemed like our roommates were gathering their belongings.

"Are you moving them?" we asked. The nurse shot back, "I can't tell you; privacy rules." We were a bit miffed at this response, but despite her attitude, our request was being fulfilled. The other family was moved to a different room, and we were given the entire room for ourselves. On that note, I flew home.

The week wasn't easy for Chaya; Nissi needed her attention twenty-four seven. At night, he'd be woken up from the variety of events going on—blood draws, medicine adjustments, or diaper changes—and would need Chaya to calm him and put him back to sleep. By Friday morning, I could tell from our phone conversation that her nerves were absolutely shot from lack of sleep. Wanting desperately to help out, I sent all the kids to friends' houses for Shabbos and bought a ticket to Boston for early that afternoon. I quickly packed up a carry-on suitcase and dashed over to the airport.

Once at the gate, I was aghast—my flight was delayed two hours, making me particularly nervous. Would I make it to Boston before Shabbos? I decided to give myself a deadline. If the plane was to take off after a certain point, I would not fly. When the pilots appeared, I told them of my dilemma. One of the pilots responded reassuringly, "We'll get you there with plenty of time before sunset." Thus relieved, I stayed, and we finally boarded the plane after 3:00 p.m. Once the plane took off, a stewardess kindly allowed me to swap seats with someone sitting up front so that as soon as the plane landed I'd be the first to exit. I sat at the edge of my seat for the duration of the flight. As soon as we parked, I sprang from my seat and dashed out of the airport as fast as I could to find a taxi. I ended up getting to the hospital for an emotional reunion with Chaya and Nissi about a half hour before Shabbos.

This gave Chaya enough time to return to the apartment we'd been given by hospitable Bostonians, take a proper shower, and begin to feel human again. Both that night and Saturday night she slept at the apartment, while I "slept" with Nissi—getting a taste of what she had dealt with the past few weeks, including waking up every time the nurse walked into the room.

Unfortunately, and despite Chaya's hope that we'd avoid it, Nissi was put on the finicky blood thinner Coumadin. That meant his blood had to be tested daily until they found the correct balance of blood fluidity. Every time a doctor would come in, poor Nissi would look up, panic-stricken, and say, "Me fine! Me fine!" It was always hard to get his veins to cooperate, so, unfortunately, he had to go through quite a few of these sessions where they'd try every trick in the book to attempt to get enough blood for testing, squeezing his arm as tight as possible, urging just a few more drops of blood to drip into the vial. Still, incredibly, he'd recover from the trauma of the procedure within seconds of its conclusion, snapping right back to happy mode. He was going to be kept on Coumadin until around the High Holidays, at the end of September.

At some point, we started talking to one of the cardiologists about the future, and how to best ensure Nissi's long-term health. He told us, "We see that the Fontan kids who do the best are the ones who exercise regularly." I told him that we were considering moving to a house with a pool, and he energetically agreed with that plan. "Firstly, water exercise is really good for these kids. But even better, when the body is in the water, it allows the organs to float, and that takes pressure off these internal organs that have been fiddled with. A pool would be an excellent idea for him." Hearing that, I promised Chaya that we would find a house with a pool.

On July 26, after three weeks in Boston, Nissi was finally ready to come home, his patchworked but powerful heart now fixed as best as possible, functioning wonderfully.

Chapter 16

A Surprise Helicopter Ride

As life returned to its normal pace, we began our search for a house with a pool that would fit within our budget. Eventually, we would locate such a house, with a large, open-floor plan—perfect for Nissi to explore the world with his gait trainer—and just two blocks from our community synagogue. After several months of negotiations with the owner, we finally got the green light to move into it toward the end of November.

But we had one more exciting episode before that. Soon after Rosh Hashanah, Nissi started coughing heavily. He barely slept one night, and we went into his room again and again to try to help, but to no avail. We decided to bring him to the pediatrician first thing in the morning.

At 9:00 a.m. on the button, as soon as the office opened, Chaya called the pediatrician. Nissi always gets first treatment, due to his complexity, so he was immediately brought into the doctor for an exam as the first patient of the day.

The physician's assistant who saw him became visibly worried, as she saw his oxygen sats dip and climb erratically. His color and energy level began to fade even as he sat on Chaya's lap. The PA made an immediate decision to call an ambulance, as she determined it was unsafe for Chaya to drive him even the few blocks to nearby Joe DiMaggio Children's Hospital without oxygen and careful monitoring.

Sure enough, Nissi got his first ambulance ride, sirens and all. He was clearly not feeling well, but he still managed to get out a few smiles between his tears.

By this time, Chaya had alerted me to what was going on, and I quickly sped to Joe DiMaggio to help out. In the meantime, the culprit was identified: Nissi had RSV again. All things considered, particularly with his level of complexity, it was decided to get him under the care of his regular cardiac team at Nicklaus Children's, about an hour's drive south of Joe DiMaggio's Children's. Once things had stabilized, while still in the emergency room, arrangements were made to transport him to Nicklaus Children's.

I called some friends to see if they could bring food for Chaya, who hadn't eaten yet that day. As we sat there talking with a doctor who was proudly wearing a kippah—who chuckled when I asked him if Nissi would be able to come home before Shabbos—two men appeared wearing flight suits. "Transport is here!" they announced. We looked at them in surprise. Transport would be on a Life Flight helicopter? "Well," said one of them, looking at Nissi, "if we'd have known he looks so good, I guess we could have taken an ambulance. But usually when we take a patient directly to the ICU, protocol mandates that we do it in a helicopter."

I laughed. There I was, an officer in the US Air Force, and my wife and almost-four-year-old were getting a helicopter ride before I ever did! They began wheeling Nissi out to the helipad. Just then, we got a call from Avigail, a teen volunteer for Chai Lifeline, that she was going to bring pizza for Chaya. We asked the pilot if he could wait a few minutes for Chaya's lunch to be dropped off, and he agreed without hesitation.

Avigail met us just outside the hospital building, and with lunch in hand, we headed to the helipad on the top floor of the garage and buckled Nissi into the colorful helicopter. Considering that Nissi was so stable, the pilot opted for a scenic flight route, so Chaya was given a beautiful aerial view of the city and the ocean, while the flight doctor took pictures out the windows. Nissi dozed on and off throughout the short flight. As for me, hearing the chopper's blades rise above me and knowing my wife and son were on that flight, gave me butterflies as I prayed for their safety and a speedy recovery for Nissi.

The flight went well, and Nissi was quickly admitted into Nicklaus Children's, where the diagnosis of RSV was confirmed. RSV can't be treated; it just needs to be waited out, so we were in for a slow ride to recovery. This time would be a lot more intense than the last time he'd caught RSV, as a one-year-old, when he was in and out of Cincinnati Children's within a single day.

The RSV vaccine is only given until age two, so this time he was not under its protective coverage. His lungs really took a hit, and he had to be put on oxygen support for a week.

On Erev Yom Kippur, already having been in the hospital for five days, we decided to bring our pre-fast meal to the hospital in an attempt to create a holiday atmosphere, despite the craziness. As the whole family marched toward his room, I saw Nissi's bed was surrounded by medical staff—never a good sign. He was having a coughing fit, which extended for two hours. Thankfully, the CPAP ventilator he was on kept him breathing through it all, until he finally recovered, dismissing everyone with an exhausted, "Me fine, me fine..." He'd have a repeat of that coughing fit a few times over Yom Kippur. Poor Chaya; her Yom Kippur was a carbon copy of her Rosh Hashanah in Boston Children's two years earlier, minus the food and her brother's company.

But, finally, he kicked the virus, and he was released from the hospital on the evening before the onset of the holiday of Sukkos, a wonderful birthday gift for me.

TOWARD THE END of that hospitalization, Dr. Rossi stopped in to say hello. At first, I didn't even recognize him, as he was wearing a suit and tie instead of his white doctor's lab coat. He laughingly apologized for his civilian attire; he had just been in a meeting with hospital donors but wanted to say hello and see how things were going. During the course of our conversation, the subject of our old friend the BT shunt came up. "How often do they clot?" I asked.

Dr. Rossi responded, "About 10 percent of the time."

I asked, "And how often do they catch the clotting?"

Dr. Rossi gave me a long look and responded, "You either have incredible luck or you have Someone watching over you. We *don't* catch it. In fact," he paused, his eyes expressing sadness, "we lost two kids just last month, here in our CICU, because of the BT shunt clotting…"

And, once again, we were dumbfounded by the open miracles Hashem has blessed us with.

IT'S AN AVERAGE EVENING IN OUR HOME. Dinner is simmering on the stove, the girls are doing homework. Chaya is on the phone with Yehuda, who is telling her about his day in yeshiva. Music is playing from the speakers in the living room. Menachi and Levi are imitating their favorite singers, microphones in hand. Nissi is in his gait trainer beside them, dancing vigorously to the tune; the springs in the contraption squeaking noisily with each exuberant jump. And the four-year-old who escaped hospice care and over a dozen other near-death experiences is singing along to the lyrics of a song from the band 8th Day. His sweet toddler voice rings out with pure joy, and even though he swaps the sound G for a D, the message is undeniably poignant:

> *In this world we only have*
> *We only have what we "dot"*
> *So "div" it, "div" it, "div" it all ya "dot"!*[1]

---

1   "All You Got," recorded by 8th Day on their album of that name. Composition and lyrics by Shmuel Marcus.

Epilogue

The first time Nissi got into the pool at our new house, comfortably heated by a heater generously funded by friends, he cried out in pure pleasure, "This is *amazing!*" And it truly is, was, and has been amazing.

Every night, as I go into his room to refill his feeding bag and see him sprawled out, sleeping softly and deeply, I think of the miracles. And every day, as he romps around the house with his gait trainer, engaging everyone in unbridled silly conversation, I thank G-d. I am absolutely positive that despite his delays, Nissi will walk unassisted one day, and with G-d's help, he will continue to grow and develop as he brings smiles to everyone he meets.

But what of those first terrifying few days of his life? People often ask me if we sued Dr. Ralph. We did speak to a few lawyers, but it was clear that, due to the vagaries of medical malpractice law, we would not win any financial settlement, for two reasons: First, thankfully and miraculously, no damages per se were caused directly by Ralph's negligence. In addition, medical malpractice cases are focused on "standard of care," and considering that the "standard care" for a child with this degree of disease is…no care whatsoever, there was no case to be won, despite the fact that we had hard evidence and testimony regarding Ralph's liability.

We opted instead to push the hospital to make changes in their protocols to make sure something like this could never happen again. I met in person with a few of the deans of pediatric medicine, as well as a member of their ethics board, and they promised me they would do an investigation. After several weeks, I got a single page letter that concluded, "We do not feel that Dr. Ralph did anything against NICU protocol."

That incensed me, so I pushed them into another investigation, providing witnesses and a comprehensive timeline of what happened. After this investigation, they gave me a full report of several pages, which admitted to "miscommunication" leading to Dr. Ralph taking full control of the case, as well as several other mistakes throughout the ordeal. But in addition to elements of the story that they reported factually incorrectly, they once again concluded that he had done nothing against protocol.

Seeing that they were only protecting him, I turned to the Washington State Medical Board. Their investigation lasted over a year, and I was shocked when they concluded that the hospital had dealt with it in-house, absolving them from any responsibility. After receiving that report, I e-mailed the deans and cc'd the president of the school, with whom I had a good relationship. I wrote that if they could not give me a list of protocols they'd changed, I was going to bring the story to the media. That got their attention.

Soon after, the deans gave me a list of changes they'd made and apologized over the phone, as much as their lawyers allowed. The changes to protocol included such basics as: in the future, a specialist would be present at the birth of any medically complex child; any individual doctor would be forbidden from taking full personal control of any case, and other such "minutiae."

At that point, I had moved on, both physically and emotionally, so I accepted it. I had other battles to fight, and I knew that was as far as we'd get.

Dr. Fern, the cardiologist who first gave us the diagnosis in utero, visited us in the hospital during Nissi's first week at Children's. Her body language revealed how worried she was that we would hold her responsible for what had happened. After all, it was her mistake—she had misread the scans and missed the clues leading to the heterotaxy diagnosis. But we weren't upset at her at all; we understood that mistakes happen. More importantly, it was she who led us into Seattle Children's in the end, so ultimately, we were appreciative of that.

We saw high-risk OB Dr. Mothers in her office for Chaya's six-week checkup after the baby was born. She was shaking like a leaf, her thin body showing a tremendous amount of apprehension as she obviously considered her own mistakes in the prenatal diagnosis. (I had never seen a doctor on the fearful side of the conversation before.) I asked her to change certain protocols in the labor and delivery ward, as well as in the high-risk clinic, and she said she would.

While we were still in her office, Teresa, one of the midwives who knew us from Yehuda's birth, saw us. She started to walk toward us, her eyes and words expressing pity. I interrupted her and told her Nissi was alive and recuperating from surgery. Her mouth dropped in utter shock and her legs gave way as she nearly fainted. Fortunately, she managed to catch herself on the receptionist's desk. Totally astounded, she somewhat pulled herself together, and after inquiring about the details, she wished us her best.

When Nissi turned four, I sent pictures of him to one of our early nurses via a mutual acquaintance. Her response read: "I am absolutely speechless. I think of him often...Such a miracle." Her next messages gave a powerful glimpse into what it must have been like from the other side of the glass, as a younger nurse with no "power" to get involved in the decisions made by those over her: "So precious and so sad. It hurts my heart...It makes me question so much—like a black hole...I'd love to know how and if they filed a lawsuit and how Dr. Ralph is still in practice...and how I didn't get dragged into it."

We were later told that Seattle Children's Hospital built a special labor and delivery room for suspected high risk births so there would be no future such "breakdowns in communication" between the two hospitals. The mother would give birth at Children's, and the baby could go straight into surgery, no intermediaries necessary. We were very gratified about that.

Obviously, we have remained deeply appreciative of the roles played by Dr. McMullan and Dr. Files, and occasionally send them pictures and notes of appreciation. When Nissi was four and a half, I realized that I hadn't written to them in a while and sent them a quick note. Dr. McMullan responded almost immediately, writing, "Nissi personifies the will to live and the will to give everyone a chance that defines humanity. I am so happy for him...and you." Dr. Files also responds regularly to our e-mail updates, one time writing: "I am always humbled by what Nissi and his family has taught me. He's not my only patient to have 'failed' palliative care, but certainly the one who has done it so spectacularly, with so much exuberance and zest for life. I can never imagine what struggles the first year of his life must have meant for you and the rest of his family, and it was never met with a complaint (that wasn't well-founded), or a desire that his life wasn't meant to be exactly as it was. Thank you for all that you have taught me, and I look forward to seeing him again someday." We have always been struck by the humility and sincerity evident in their words.

And Dr. Ralph? We e-mailed back and forth to each other a few times. I told him—without mincing any words—that the only reason why I could imagine everything had happened the way it did was to magnify the miracle, and hopefully to inspire him to a greater recognition of G-d's capabilities. I even suggested several things he could do if he felt bad for his behavior toward us. In his responses to me, it was clear that he had lawyered up and would not take responsibility for his treatment of us. I wish his mind and soul a speedy recovery.

As for us, at this point, we are beyond grateful for where things are at. Nissi continues to grow, to laugh, and to thrive. Our feelings can only be best expressed through chapter 30 of *Tehillim*:

> *A psalm; a song of dedication of the House of David. I will exalt You, G-d, for You have raised me up, and You have not allowed my enemies to rejoice over me.*
>
> **The Hebrew word for "raised me up," dilisani, also means "made me impoverished." The nineteenth-century sage the Sfas Emes beautifully explains[1] this linguistic conundrum by pointing out that the word dli means a bucket. A bucket is lowered into the deep darkness of the well but for the purpose of raising up life-giving water. Likewise, we thank G-d even for experiences of "being lowered into poverty"**

---

1 *Sfas Emes* on *Tehillim*, loc. cit.

since they are for the purpose of raising us higher, giving us gifts we'd never have otherwise known...

G-d, I have cried out to You, and You have healed me. G-d, You have brought my soul from the grave; You have revived me from my descent into the grave. Sing to G-d, His pious ones, and give thanks to His holy Name. For His wrath lasts but a moment; life results from His favor; in the evening, I lie down weeping, but in the morning, there is joyful singing.

As a nine-year-old child, Rabbi Dovber of Lubavitch explained this verse: "When one would like 'roga,' calm, he should conw template that 'G-d truly wants life!' Then, the tears of return to G-d will bring one to the joy of Divine revelation."[2]

And I said in my tranquility, "I will never falter." G-d, with Your will, You set up my mountain to be might, You hid Your countenance and I became frightened. To You, G-d, I would call, and to G-d I would supplicate, "What gain is there in my blood, in my descent to the grave? Will dust thank You; will it recite Your truth?"

How many times did I say these words in desperate prayer before Nissi was born?! I'd pray, "Allow this child to live so we can recite Your truth!"

Hear, G-d, and be gracious to me; G-d, be my helper.

And in the end, G-d indeed heard our prayers.

You have turned my lament into dancing for me; You loosened my sackcloth and girded me with joy.

And I tell this story, again and again, to fulfill my promise.

So that my soul will sing praises to You and not be silent. G-d, my G-d, I will thank You forever.

---

2   *Sefer Hama'amarim* 5700, p. 44.

Part II

REFLECTIONS *for* MEDICAL PERSONNEL, FAMILIES, *and* FRIENDS

Thoughts for Medical Professionals

O ne evening, I retold this story for an online crowd. Afterward, during the question-and-answer session, one of the listeners spoke up. She said, "I'm a doctor myself. When I went to medical school, we were told that medicine is 80 percent science and 20 percent art. I feel that we've lost the art of medicine."

With those thought-provoking words, we'd like to reflect on our medical journey. We've been privileged to see and experience some phenomenal medical practitioners, but we have also been brought into awful places of pain as a result of people who have lost the "art" of medicine. The art of medicine is everything a machine is not: warm, compassionate, and personal. The cold information that science provides must be tempered and curated by the empathy and humanity of the doctor, and directed by G-dly morality.

What follows are ideas that would, in our opinion, help change hospitals from "Places for the Ill" into "Places of Healing," and provide some insight into the "art of healing" of which that doctor spoke. Many of these ideas are extrapolations from the Rebbe's approach to healing,[1] from his writings or stories told about him. Others are culled from our personal experiences, but are inspired by the writ and wisdom of Judaism and Chassidic philosophy.

---

1   For an extensive treatment of this subject, see *Healthy in Body, Mind and Spirit*, ch. 6.

THE REBBE WOULD OFTEN QUOTE or paraphrase his prede-
cessor, the Tzemach Tzedek, "Doctors were given permission by G-d to
heal, not to cause a crestfallen spirit [by predicting]."[2]

This statement holds within it the mission statement of every medical professional: You are a healer. Your job is to heal. When one enters
a patient's room with that objective, the relationship is different. There
is a connection, a purpose, and a mission. All this is alluded to in the
term the Rebbe created for hospitals—*"beis refuah,"* a place of healing.

But one other point in the Tzemach Tzedek's statement is just as crucial. As a medical professional, you have been granted *partnership* with
G-d. When one looks at it that way, the profession becomes a spiritual
one, and the experiences are humbling.

We can contrast that with a quip told to me by Rabbi Mordechai
Farkash, after I told this story in his Chabad House. "The Talmud comments, 'The best of doctors are destined to purgatory.'[3] One way of
understanding that is by looking at the Hebrew word for "the best" in
that phrase, *tov,* which has the numerical value of seventeen. There are
some doctors who think that for them, there should be only seventeen
blessings in the *Amidah,* instead of eighteen. They say, 'I do not need
to make the blessing of *Refaeinu,* asking G-d to heal the sick, because
that's what I do. I don't need G-d's help.' Such doctors are destined for
purgatory..."

All jokes aside, we have noticed that the very best doctors are exceedingly humble. They allow G-d to work through their hands, and they
recognize that life is truly a Divine gift, which they have been privileged
to study and interact with. Chassidic philosophy reflects on the power
of humility versus the distraction of ego. When one nullifies their ego,
they allow themselves to tap into energies and capabilities that they

---

2   Here's one of many examples of the Rebbe's letters in this vein: "With regard to a particular
     situation—it is impossible to know clearly and with certainty [about the eventual outcome].
     Clearly, the pronouncement of the doctor that the situation is hopeless is definitely out
     of place. At the very most he can say—and indeed all that a human being is capable of
     saying—that he does not take responsibility for the future, but [he can say] no more than
     that." *Igros Kodesh* Vol. 20, p. 183.

3   *Kiddushin* 4:14.

didn't know exist. Ego, on the other hand, distracts and interferes by placing one's self as the center of every experience. The greatest musicians are able to let go of themselves on stage and allow the music itself to take over; their own sense of self dissipates as they dissolve into something greater than themselves. When we become completely focused on something Above, we put "ourselves" aside, and that's where the magic happens.

The Rebbe's treatment of the Tzemach Tzedek's quote also defines what doctors are *not*, and that is crucial: doctors are not fortune tellers or forecasters. There are several important lessons to glean from this, particularly with regards to modern medicine.

Firstly, statistics are only useful in clarifying and stratifying what has happened in the past. They have little practical relevance on the individual case before you because we do not yet know on which side of the statistics the person will fall into. In our first conversation together, Dr. McMullan expressed this idea very well. He said, "If there is a 99 percent chance of fatality, and a 1 percent chance at life—if this child is in the 1 percent, he will 100 percent live." Statistics are only useful for deciding the best avenues of healing, but they cannot predict definitively *what will happen.*

There is a fantastic story told of a conversation between the Rebbe and one of his cardiologists, shortly after his heart attack in 1978. The doctor told the Rebbe, "If you don't take care of yourself, there is a 25 percent chance of recurrence of the heart attack. Do you understand?" And the Rebbe wittily responded, "Yes; you said that even if I *don't* take care of myself, there is a 75 percent chance I'll be fine!"[4]

When we found ourselves in the labor and delivery ward about to give birth to Yehuda, a doctor came in and began to "regale" us with a twenty-six-week preemie's chances of survival and all the negative possibilities that existed. I interrupted her and said, "Those statistics aren't going to help us any. You focus on what you need to do, and we'll do what we need to do. And let G-d's plan work itself out." Amazingly,

---

4   See https://www.chabad.org/therebbe/article_cdo/aid/60696/jewish/health/htm.

Yehuda beat every one of the odds he was put against and is today a perfectly healthy teenager. The statistics were absolutely irrelevant for us.

In fact, had we known the actual odds he was up against, we would have been under far greater stress, and it is likely that would have *lessened* our ability to create a healing and growing environment for him. And that's another key lesson: By attaching too much value to the statistics, one creates a self-fulfilling prophecy, sort of the mirror image of the placebo effect. One should consider the power of encouragement versus discouragement when presenting information, while maintaining the effort to convey the reality of the situation.

Statistics also don't take into account the future, with the advent of new medication and technologies. Soon after Nissi was born, a prestigious cardiologist told my father, "Tell your son that they need to get through the first year. After that, they shouldn't worry; the world of cardiology changes every six months due to all the new technology being developed." That's also true of many other medical fields.

Don't get bogged down by statistics—that type of data is static and distracts from the art of healing. There must be a balance between letting people know about the path ahead, difficulties included, without piling it all on. A good doctor will understand how to find that comfortable balance.

Additionally, when doctors give "time limits" on people's lives, they create a reality in the mind of the patient that shouldn't exist: that of finality. Nothing is absolute, as discussed earlier. But in any case, the patient should be encouraged to live out the entirety of the rest of his or her life with purpose and meaning—be it a day, a week, or longer. Every moment is valuable; why spend it in fear?

Besides, medical professionals must also remember that each individual patient is slightly different, whether in the mind or muscle. There are those who might succumb to minor problems, and there are those who have the inner strength and drive to overcome even the "impossible." A good doctor should find a way to encourage his or her patients to be in the latter category.

There are those who contend that this approach allows for "false hope." I find that exasperating; by definition, hope means that there is a chance for failure. Why can't medical professionals be cognizant of the optimistic possibilities, if at all possible? Why do they need to be constantly focused on the negative?

The Rebbe wrote about this conundrum, saying (emphasis added): "Care should be taken not to *exaggerate* expectations through far-fetched promises, for false hopes inevitably result in deep disenchantment, loss of credibility, and other undesirable effects. However, a way can surely be found to avoid raising false hopes, yet giving *guarded encouragement*."[5]

Based on these ideas, we can see that it is extremely important to avoid making absolute statements about what will happen. In this book, we mentioned our experiences with a medical fellow who told us in no uncertain terms that Nissi would need a fundoplication to stop his reflux. In the end, the medically proficient doctor was wrong. That happens far more often than most patients realize. In our opinion, things need to be framed in such a way that the patient knows that there are *possibilities*, and what the *expected results* of the possibilities are. When doctors become hyper-focused on diagnoses and prognoses, they lose sight of the ultimate goal of healing.

To this end, medical professionals also need to be careful to give relevant information without overwhelming the patient or family. Blowing people away with your extensive knowledge is not constructive or appreciated. We had one experience like that with our preemie, Yehuda. A surgeon decided to overwhelm us with her knowledge, providing us with an overload of information, and no information on the status of our child. We were infuriated, and she was later swapped out for another surgeon who explained things—after complimenting us on our baby!—in clear and simple terms.

Simplify and convey the information in layers, even spread across several conversations. Parents are overwhelmed enough as it is. After the three-hour prenatal scans, we were given half a year's worth of

---

5   Letter to Prof. Robert Wilkes, 1979, printed in *My Story*, p. 192. While that extraordinarily valuable letter deals specifically with the issues related to children with mental ailments, its messages apply equally to any area of healing.

anatomy and biology lessons in a twenty-minute crash course. Between the complexity of the disease and the swirling emotions, is there any wonder we were overloaded? Instead, focus on the major concerns and courses of action, and don't get lost in the weeds. Consider only the information that is absolutely necessary. If the parents need more information, they'll ask for it.

The way you frame information has incredible importance. The Rebbe taught us to be extremely mindful of the words we use. I met a surgeon who, when talking about the surgery he planned to do, spoke about "taking out chunks of meat." This inspired no confidence in his skill. Rather, his cavalier attitude spoke of his lack of compassion. Why would we want to use a surgeon like that?

Bedside manner is important. The person in front of you, your patient, is vulnerable. They need strength. You can provide them with strength by the attitude you profess. One doctor told me, "When I was in medical school, they said, 'Would you rather have a nice surgeon, or a good surgeon?' I raised my hand and said, 'Why can't we have both?!'" It is a false narrative that you must create a barrier between yourself and your patient. A good doctor knows where to find the balance so that he or she can lead the patient to a healthier place.

There is yet another area in the medical field that needs to be addressed. The Rebbe was worried about the advent of computers in hospitals. Not that they shouldn't be used, but that medical professionals should ensure that despite the valuable information computers provide, the doctors must remain focused on the patient. The fear, as he expressed to Dr. Mordechai Shani,[6] was that doctors would lose their connection with their patients, thereby missing out on key possibilities of healing. And that's critical. To put it in simpler terms: the technical diagnosis, prognosis, and test results can distract from the clinical reality, which is what is seen in proximity to the patient, by physical sense, and not just via computer screens. This is—in part—what led to the first surreal and traumatic days after Nissi's birth: a doctor who was

---

6   See www.chabad.org/therebbe/livingtorah/player_cdo/aid/3323934/jewish/patient-empowerment-htm.

dogmatically stuck on the prognosis, to the point that he lost the plot and was ignoring the clinical reality—a child who was not only alive, but stable enough to be a candidate for surgery.

It is, of course, true that sometimes there is nothing for you to do. The reality is that there will be many cases in which the patient's illness is beyond the capabilities of the medical world. But healing can still be done—the patient can be surrounded with love and concern, and medical staff can focus on making the rest of the person's life as comfortable and happy as possible. Palliative and hospice care have their time and place. But people should certainly not be pushed into their hands the way we were!

And while tragically you obviously can't save every patient, the knowledge that you fought your best combined with the humble recognition that G-d is truly running the show will keep you grounded and emotionally fit to continue your chosen profession.

Thoughts for Families in Medical Crises

Y ou've been thrown into a situation that you were never prepared for, and certainly never wanted. Life will, in all probability, never be the same. What do you do?

While everyone may have different coping mechanisms—all in accordance with their lifestyle, belief system, and character traits—here are some thoughts taken from our experiences, written with the heartfelt hope that others will find them useful in finding healthy crisis management that fits their own unique situation.

First, a few mindsets that kept us going. These ideas had been part of our life long in advance of this experience. We somehow made them part of our daily routine to the point that they became automatic guidance points for us, spiritual orientation tools. Simple reflection on these concepts, even for a few seconds a day, proved beyond invaluable to us.

- As Jews, we say *Shema* twice daily. On a simple level, we are stating that there is only one G-d. But on a deeper level, we are affirming that in truth, everything is G-d. There is nothing outside of G-d. Cognizance of this truth lifted us up. It reminded us that we were created by G-d and are kept alive by G-d—and so is this child.

- The special relationship between G-d and every individual was described by Rabbi Israel Baal Shem Tov as even greater than the love between an only child born to parents in their old age. Chaya and I took two elements out of this idea. First, Chaya felt the strength of leaning on G-d. Her heart said, "G-d, you love me as a parent loves a child, and therefore I know I can trust that what I'm going through is what's best for me, even if I don't feel it." Second, during our ordeal, our prayers became plaintive and straight from the heart. They weren't extravagant; just simple and absolutely raw.

I remember thinking, "G-d, this is all I've got. Please take it." In retrospect, I look on those prayers as being possibly equivalent to a *minchas ani*, a pauper's gift to G-d, which, despite its lack of adornments, is beloved by G-d due to its sincerity and wholesomeness. I do not pretend any holiness or depth of spiritual feeling at the time. I had nothing of the sort. All that remained was simple: "G-d, you created me, and you put me in this situation. Please help."

- When we asked for help, we took our lead from Chana, the mother of the prophet Samuel. She did not ask for herself; she asked that her prayers be answered *for G-d's own sake*. Likewise, we begin the thrice-daily *Amidah* prayer with the statement, "G-d, open my lips, and my mouth shall declare Your praise."[1] Noting that the proper place for such a declaration should be at the very beginning of prayer, the Rebbe explains that prayer until this point should have brought one to a state of self-nullification.[2] As such, the requests we make in the *Amidah* are no longer for our personal needs or desires, but for the purpose of declaring G-d's praise. Likewise, we asked G-d's assistance with our child, not for ourselves but for the purpose of expressing G-d's praises.

- Sometime prior to this experience, I came across an unbelievable idea in a Chassidic discourse from the Rebbe.[3] In it, he explains that the Hebrew word "*nes*" has several meanings: a miracle, a challenge, and a banner. The three unrelated homonyms then express a powerful message: The *purpose* of a challenge is to *lift*

---

1   Samuel 1:11.
2   *Toras Menachem Sefer Hama'amarim* 5711–12, p. 257.
3   Ibid., p. 332.

you up (like a banner). We *overcome* challenges by *lifting ourselves higher*. And the meaning of *challenges*, as is the purpose of *miracles*, is to show the inner truth of the world—nothing exists besides G-d. This concept reverberated in my mind throughout the experience.

- "You don't know how strong you are until being strong is the only choice you have." Chaya saw this message on a cardiac awareness bumper sticker, and, uncharacteristically, she felt compelled to buy it and display it on her car. Every time people tell us they are impressed by our strength, we quote them our bumper sticker (although a quick internet search credits it to Bob Marley).

That pithy line has its philosophical sources in Jewish theology. The Talmud tells us that G-d only gives us what we can handle.[4] Honestly, sometimes that statement feels...well, at the least, unrelatable. (And though they mean well, it can even feel downright infuriating when someone tells you, "Boy, you must really be able to handle a lot; after all..." We can come to that discovery of our inner strengths ourselves, but what we need from others is empathy, not their assumption that we can handle what we've been given.)

The following paraphrase of an insight from Rabbi Yosef Yitzchak Schneerson of Lubavitch allowed me, personally, to come to terms with it:

> Our Sages say that "one is obligated to say the world was created for me."[5] The word for world, *olam*, has four distinct meanings in Hebrew: a physical world, concealment, youthful strength, and time. The message in this statement is now deeper and richer: I am obligated to consider and reflect upon my world and to recognize that any seeming negativity that I see at any particular place and time was created for me to uncover the G-dliness hidden within it. At the very same time, within that "concealment" is also locked the strength that

---

4   *Kesubos* 67a.

5   *Sanhedrin,* 37a.

> *I have been given to uncover the inner truth—that it is but*
> *a facade over the G-dliness that enlivens it all.*[6]

- Within the struggles of fighting for a child's life, there is one particularly dangerous emotion that can—understandably—arise, but must be avoided at all cost: anger. The Rebbe told pediatrician Dr. Stuart Ditchek the following: "If you are angry at G-d because of a diagnosis, you are hurting the chance that this child has for a miracle."[7] Frustration? Certainly. Our prayers are full of expressing frustration; we continuously ask G-d to change things as they are. But *anger* is quite different; it is a destructive flame. It sends us into the spiral of despair instead of into the depths of our souls and to the innermost connection with G-d. That space is the place of our core strength, and, when G-d wills it, is also the place from where miracles spring forth. But it doesn't deny the pain; it acknowledges the struggle. As King David writes about G-d (in Psalms 91:15), "I am with him in trouble and pain." Anger will create but distance when we need to be as close as possible.

- Finally, here are three meditations that Chaya has found very valuable: First, let go of the past—you can't do anything about it. Second, let go of the future—you haven't gotten there. And third, focus on here and now—because that's all we can control. So much of our stress is from our pain of the past and fear of the future. By eliminating the cold grip they have over us, we release ourselves to make the most of the present.

Ultimately, it really comes down to this: despite the difficulty inherent in doing so, we need to control and direct our thoughts and emotions, because otherwise, they will distract us from the battle ahead. Most important is to trust G-d and remain positive, not just because that gives us the strength to proceed, but because it creates Divine channels for blessing. When we allow ourselves to fall into despair, we lose sight

---

6   *Igrot Kodesh Rayatz*, vol. 2, p. 248.
7   JEM interview with Dr. Ditchek: https://bit.ly/30EFnPT.

of our goals and allow ourselves to fall victim to the disease. Practically speaking, it interferes with our ability to project strength, direction, and fighting spirit to the sick child and to the medical team. You want them to be fighting with you. Your trust, optimism, and projection of calm will definitely influence their attitudes.

IN ADDITION TO THE MINDSETS we used to fuel ourselves, we knew that we needed to have a practical as well as a spiritual action plan.

Two words come to mind immediately: strategize and stratify.

In my military training, I learned that strategy doesn't just mean planning out what we need to do to win the battles. Strategy is also a matter of predicting what would have happened if everything went wrong. Identify your worst-case scenario and look backward. What would have happened to get you there? For us, the worst-case scenario would be that the stress caused by the sickness would pull the family apart. Unfortunately, illness in the family is one of the major causes for divorce. So the very forefront of our strategy was to maintain the stability of our family as best as possible.

The center of every family is the husband-wife/mother-father unit. When a child is hospitalized, that unit is stretched thin. We must recognize that the unit is made up of two: each person as an individual, with different coping mechanisms and stress barometers, as well as the two together, united as parents. Both of these sides of ourselves need careful tending.

On the individual level: with the sick child demanding all attention, care of our spouse is often forgotten. Chaya and I worked hard to make sure we were supporting each other, putting in extra effort to be aware of each other's feelings at any time, particularly when the goings were rough. We tried to pay extra attention to each other and notice if the other seemed burned out, and we would encourage each other to take a break, get some food, go out with friends, or sleep in. Also, a small surprise gift or gesture goes a long way during difficult times.

But the husband-wife unit must not be abandoned. We did our best to nurture our togetherness. No matter the circumstances, we tried to end our evenings together in a calm space—whether it was through a quiet walk, playing low-key board games, or watching unemotional documentaries. In addition, when things had stabilized a bit, we rented a beautiful getaway for a single night. It was extremely valuable for us to drop the tension and spend time together, alone, if even for short periods of time.

"Care for the caretaker" cannot be overestimated. You can only do your best if you have a space to find tranquility. Each person is different; all our needs differ. But make sure your needs are met (spiritual, emotional, and physical—don't forget food, showers, sleep—and chocolate!) so you can be fully charged.

Above all else, do not allow the guilt of not caring properly for yourself, your spouse, or your children to overcome you. Rather, set small goals in each area that *can* be accomplished. With each small success, you will feel more strength and capacity to set larger goals. But it can start with something as small as a coffee date with your spouse or a nice long shower for yourself.

We are often asked how we dealt with the rest of our children during this challenging period. First, I learned from my parents that while children do not need to know all the details, they should feel some involvement in the healing process. We did that by bringing them to the hospital, encouraging them to show Nissi their love. When Nissi's brothers and sisters came to visit him, they did it with joy and excitement, running down the CICU, sanitizing their hands, and then crowding around Nissi's bed. We encouraged them to ask questions about the monitors and machinery in order to remove any sense of fear they may have had. Before leaving at night, they would chorus *Shema* together—and kiss him, one by one.

In fact, they became so much part and parcel of the hospital experience that they were featured in a brochure that Seattle Children's Hospital produced for families called "What to Expect When You Visit Your Sibling in the NICU." Pictures of them were taken (kippahs perched at impossible angles on Levi's and Menachi's heads, their tzitzis flying) as they proceeded through each element of visitation. The staff loved them; many of the nurses—and even the receptionist!—referred to them as "my children," and would ask about them on a regular basis. But when things were rocky, we kept them away from the hospital.

We did our best to stick to routines, and to give the children as much normal attention as possible. When Nissi was a baby, it was much easier for us to leave him in the hospital overnight in the care of the nurses, which allowed us to keep up the bedtime routine at home. But as a toddler, we found he needed us much more, and was often in a different city, so one parent was always at his side. That proved to be very challenging, as we were both maxing out much faster. We relied heavily on family and friends to step in and care for our kids. But in order to make it as easy as possible, we tried to give the kids new toys around that time so they had something special and exciting to focus on for themselves.

Throughout, we made sure to occasionally speak to each child individually to try to get a sense of his or her fears or worries, and even communicated the situation with their teachers. I believe our children did so well because they knew that we were aware of their needs, despite everything. As we often tell them, "If G-d forbid *you* were sick, we would spend the same effort to make sure *you* were taken care of." Finally, when we were under tremendous stress, we would apologize for and explain our exhaustion so they would not take it personally. As a result of our frankness with them, they sometimes even tried to take care of us!

The next element is stratify: What can I control, and what am I not able to control? What is critical for the moment, and what elements of life can be dropped off for right now? Some things are just not crucial when in crisis mode, and every family will have its own list. For us, homework and grades went out the window. We simply had no energy left for them.

A few other helpful tips:

- **Delegate to others as much as possible.** Save your energy and time for things of immediate importance. Write things down and keep a running list of the things you need so you can respond immediately when someone asks what they can do for you.

- **Don't hide your situation from your community.** Let others know what you are facing so they can step up and help out. We received a tremendous amount of physical, emotional, and even financial support once news of our situation got out—and, to be honest, we were not planning on releasing it for "public consumption" and had even considered keeping it private. Had we not allowed it to be publicized, we feel that we would have quite possibly drowned in the tidal wave of problems we were up against. People have the mitzvah, the responsibility, of *gemilus chassadim*, acts of kindness; allow them to access that mitzvah on your behalf!

- **Reach out for help.** There is a plethora of incredible organizations that will help you through your ordeal. But the key is to reach out for help—you will certainly be better off when you do. Don't be a martyr; save your energy for where it's needed most. Isolating your specific needs will help you hone in on the resources that will help you most.

- **Whenever possible, get rest.** We opted not to sleep in the hospital during the first five months, and that was crucial for us. Nissi was safe with the nurses, and we were able to be functional parents at the same time. Later, as he got older and needed us present, we would take turns sleeping with him, enabling us to get some sleep some of the time, as sleeping in the hospital only happens in short spurts. Still, other people might have a different approach. A friend with a child with cardiac disease felt it was absolutely necessary for them to have someone stay with their child at all times. While that may be true for you, it is undoubtedly of utmost importance to occasionally spend time outside the hospital in order to regroup mentally and emotionally. The hospital garden is a great start; we loved the rooftop garden at Boston Children's. But as difficult as it may be, do whatever you can to see the outside world every so often and thereby refresh yourself. Sometimes, a friend or family member can be found to relieve you for a few hours. That's not abandonment—that's making you a better caregiver.

- **Create a positive atmosphere in the hospital room** by bringing in décor that is appropriate. Sterility is boring, boring is exhausting, and exhausting is not healing. Make the room a friendly place—without going overboard.
- **Don't forget to eat.** Sounds simple, but it's not. Hospital time seems to operate as if on a different planet, and an entire day can go by without even thinking of food. At the very least, have high protein snacks available at the hospital so you can keep yourself going. Don't underestimate how beneficial ordering takeout or asking a friend to bring a hot meal can be.
- **Celebrate holidays in a way that they maintain their energy, happiness, and spirituality.** This can be very difficult, but it is an absolute necessity. We did whatever we could: I sang through *Kabbalas Shabbos* at home as if I were leading the prayers. I danced with my children while singing *Lecha Dodi*. The songs I sang at the Shabbos table pulled me out of the weekly grind; and while it took effort to sing them, the catharsis they brought me was worth it. We made sure to buy the children something special for the holidays. The other children, and you yourself(!), *need* the holiday atmosphere. Do whatever it takes to keep what they expect for Shabbos and holidays, even though, of course, there will be differences. The same holds true, to whatever degree you are able to do so, even within the hospital itself.
- **Recognize that things change.** These experiences truly change us, whether or not we like it. After Nissi was discharged, I made an attempt to take a real hike—three mountainous miles—to a spot that had been on our wish list for quite a while in the nearby Cascade Mountains. As I recounted earlier in this book, it was not relaxing at all and, in fact, was rather stressful. Later, when we went to Hawaii, we still tried to enjoy adventure. No dice. It took a while for us to learn that we would need to shift away from the things that had previously brought us calm and relaxation and find new vistas. It might be sad to do so, but we need to embrace the change and go with it. Don't allow yourself to get stuck in the past—it's not constructive.

- **Don't be afraid to tell well-meaning people your limits.** Set visiting times and limits. Don't feel bad; if they are truly trying to assist you, they will appreciate knowing what you need and don't need. In any case, you deserve the right to tell them what works for you and what doesn't.

REGARDING SPECIFIC ACTIONS that one should take, here are some things the Rebbe would often suggest to those facing medical challenges. The Rebbe was a master of both spirituality as well as practicality, and his advice to those in crisis reflects both of those elements. Let's begin with the practical:

- Get a second opinion. You need to find a doctor who is bullish on the odds of recovery, someone willing to take on the case and fight with you, as a team.
- Speak to a doctor who is a friend—someone who has *your* interests in mind.
- If you have several doctors' opinions, go with the majority.
- Always look for the best specialists.

In order to receive spiritual assistance, we need to widen the channel of Divine flow by fostering a greater and stronger relationship with G-d. Here are suggestions made by the Rebbe for Jewish families to fit that bill:[8]

- **Check your mezuzos and tefillin.** Make sure all the doors on your house have mezuzos and that they are in the right place.
- **Find an area in Torah and mitzvos that you and your family can refine.**
- **Give charity.** Giving charity has protective and healing power in and of itself, as the Prophet Daniel suggested to King Nebuchadnezzar.[9] King Solomon wrote unambiguously, "Charity saves from death."[10] Giving charity is advice that the Rebbe gave

---

8   For extensive treatment of this subject, see *Healthy in Body, Mind and Spirit*, ch. 8.
9   *Daniel* 4:24.
10   Proverbs 10:2.

numerous people in crises, often telling women that they should give charity prior to lighting Shabbos candles Friday night, and telling men to give charity every day before prayers. But he also suggested that a charity box be placed in the hospital room of the patient. Whether that was for easy access to giving charity or as a reminder to do so regularly, I am not sure.

- **Do a physical action that expresses your belief in a positive outcome.** Take positivity to the next level by doing a physical action to demonstrate your absolute belief that G-d will hear your prayers, for example, by making a joyous Kiddush, putting a down payment for a *seudas hoda'ah*, or the like. We did something similar with Yehuda's birth—we bought a stroller that sat quietly in our house for three months until he finally came home in it. With Nissi's birth, our seven-seater minivan became too small for our family. In the hope and belief that Nissi would survive, we took ownership of an eight-seater minivan. It was a way of demonstrating our belief and trust in G-d with a physical decision—grounding it, giving it something for a theoretical, spiritual blessing to "grab hold of" within this world.

- **Use the element of joy.** A close friend of mine has a son who went through an extremely complicated heart surgery. The repair failed several times during the operation, resulting in the procedure taking an incredible eighteen hours. After completing *Tehillim* for the umpteenth time that day, my friend thought to himself, *The only tool I have left is joy. There is a Chassidic saying*[11] *that joy breaks all boundaries.* And with that, he stood up, started singing a particularly energetic Chassidic tune, and began dancing. Shortly afterward, he was happily informed that the surgeons were finishing up and had finally succeeded with the repair. What can you do to access joy, even in impossible situations? It certainly means reaching deep into your core, to the very source of life. Consider deeply that the world and therein

---

11   *Sefer Hama'amarim* 5657, p. 223.

is but G-d's domain, and that we are privileged to serve Him in a unique manner. This detaches us from our worries and fears and connects us directly with the One Above.

- **Remember that you are placed in any situation, even a hospitalization, for a Divine purpose.** Early in our story, I complained to Chaya, expressing my frustration that I simply was not able to accomplish my *shlichus*, my mission, on campus—the reason we were living so far away from family and friends in the first place. Chaya wisely responded, "Who's to say that's your *shlichus* now?" In fact, we took on our medical situation as a spiritual responsibility in and of itself. Our social media posts reflected the positivity we wanted to project in any situation, demonstrating a Jew's approach to adversity. People bought into Nissi's story because everyone loves a scrappy little fighter, an underdog. And we didn't hesitate to share every little success, the tiniest victories, trying to exhibit that there's *always* good news. We also did our best to have a positive influence on the hospital staff, and even, when the situation allowed for it, fellow parents. And, of course, we asked people to take on mitzvos for Nissi, including the surgical staff. We know of several people who actually made life changes—some *kashering* their kitchens, others becoming Shabbos observant—in Nissi's merit!

- **Learn daily.** The Rebbe would often tell people to begin studying the daily study cycles of *Chitat: Chumash*—one *aliyah* of the weekly *parashah* in accordance with the day (Sunday—*Rishon*, etc.); *Tehillim*, as it was split up in the thirty-day cycle; and *Tanya*, in accordance with its yearly cycle. Later, the study of Maimonides' *Mishneh Torah* was added, with the daily cycles of one chapter, three chapters, or the yearly cycle of *Sefer Hamitzvos*. No matter one's study level, having a spiritual minimum standard that we do not drop below, no matter the circumstances, is an amazing way to keep one's stability and sanity in the midst of crisis.

- **Study works that focus on trusting in G-d** no matter what the circumstances. The eleventh-century work *Chovos Halevavos* has a section titled *Shaar Habitachon,* and the Rebbe often told people to study it to strengthen their trust and belief in G-d. A famous section of the classic *Tanya, Igeres Hakodesh,* chapter eleven, focuses on the subject of suffering in light of the statement that "evil does not descend from G-d." And the Rebbe's own letters, found in over forty volumes in several languages, deal with the subjects of faith and trust extensively. I found a bit of serenity by reading a few of the Rebbe's letters every night before going to sleep.

- **Pray at holy sites.** The Rebbe himself would often offer his blessings to people in the form of his short statement: "I will mention you at the resting place of my father-in-law." At every juncture, we did our best to make sure that the Rebbe was informed of the goings-on—my brother-in-law Mendy was our go-to, and he went to the Rebbe's gravesite often during those months, and even afterward.

- **Communicate the good news when it's available.** Appreciation of the blessings as they come is a critical part of the process. In a letter to one of his foremost followers, the Rebbe wrote, "Think for a moment: Before the operation, you wrote many times, [sending] requests, [asking] that the operation be successful. When G-d fulfilled the blessing of my revered, sainted father-in-law, the Rebbe, and the operation was successful, you did not share these tidings. Now you report that you are again aggrieved concerning her general health. According to my understanding, the proper order should be: (a) first give thanks to G-d for His great kindness in the past, then (b) a prayer, combined with utter trust, that G-d will continue granting His blessings, and her situation will continue to improve. Faith and trust are immensely powerful catalysts to influence and bring about revealed and apparent good..."[12]

---

12 *Igrot Kodesh,* vol. 3, p. 394.

- **Tap into the power of *Tehillim*.** In addition to all the above, this piece of advice almost goes without saying: The Tzemach Tzedek said, "If one would know the power of reciting *Tehillim*, they'd say it all day."[13] We had friends and family on various Whatsapp groups splitting up *Tehillim* during every crisis. We are certain all those prayers had a powerful impact.

---

13 *Hayom Yom*, 24 Shevat.

Thoughts for Friends
of Families Going through
Medical Crises

As we've noted, we benefited greatly from the support of our friends and family. Over time, we also learned what elements of assistance were particularly effective for us and what wasn't helpful. With regard to the latter, our experience was that many people simply did not know what to do to help or how to express their concern. Based on our observations, here are a few tips on how friends and community can best help families in crisis:

- **Communicate your concern.** If you're thinking about the person, drop them a line and let them know that. Text or Whatsapp messages are invaluable. Even if the parents do not respond, know that your concern is felt and appreciated.
- **Offer specific help.** While general questions such as "What can I do to help?" are well-meaning, for a family in crisis this ends up being yet another overwhelming question that needs to be addressed. Instead, offer tangible and concrete assistance: "I'm going to the grocery store; what kinds of cereal do your children eat? Can I get you bread, fruit, or any other staples?" The practical offer gives the person in crisis an idea of how indeed you can help them, while the vague offer often gets the unrealistic, and probably untrue, response, "Everything's fine." In addition, a few pointed questions will help you pinpoint the best way you

can help this particular family. Asking what they like for supper, when is a good time to send over cleaning help, or similar questions eliminate any need for decision-making to an already overwhelmed family.

- **Express concern for the caregiver, not just the sick family member.** When caring for a sick family member, the caregivers often put their own needs last. It's okay to ignore the patient for a little while and focus on the exhausted, harried, stressed-out, and emotionally spent parent or caregiver. By giving them strength with your friendship and care, you will benefit the patient as well.

  To quote a good friend of ours, Dr. Sarah Stroup, "Understand that the parents and caregivers are also patients. We are also suffering. Treat us kindly. Deal with our silence. Deal with our anger. Deal with our outbursts. Deal with what may seem like antisocial behavior—because guess what: we're not feeling too social, and we may have special difficulty around those who have healthy children. We may resent them. That is our right. We are ill too. We are doing our best…cut us some slack."

  Some helpful ideas and always-appreciated gestures are gift cards of any sort, babysitting and cleaning help, dinners, groceries, toys for the siblings, small gifts for the caregivers, cash, respite care, and meal trains.

- **Be sensitive in conversation.** Sometimes people are overly positive because they can't handle the intensity of the situation, so they try to reassure primarily themselves—and only by extension the family in crisis—by nervously making comments such as "It's going to be okay" or "He's doing better now, right?" Make sure that your messages of positivity and hope are sensitive to the feelings of the family. Families going through medical situations or dealing with a special-needs child are experiencing very deep emotions, even if they don't show it outwardly. Those who are blessed with good health cannot begin to imagine the life of a special-needs family—the chaos that can erupt at a moment's notice, the never-ending work to keep hospitalizations at bay, and the sheer emotional exhaustion from it all. Your appreciation of the magnitude of these and other challenges—not in a heroic way, but with an eye toward reality—will be greatly welcome. Common expressions like "I know what you mean" can be painful to a caregiver under the pressure of life-and-death decisions. Train yourself to replace it with "I can't even imagine" or similar. Unsolicited advice, whether regarding the patient, other children, or even the parents themselves may not only be not appreciated but may even be hurtful. Anything that smacks of criticism strikes deep to those in a vulnerable state. The difference between sympathy and empathy is of utmost importance. Sympathy is when you feel bad for the other person. Empathy is when you join the other to *share* their burden. Validate instead of relate. And most importantly, find ways to encourage and support without being intrusive.

- **Don't probe for information.** The caregivers will convey whatever they feel comfortable sharing.

- **Leave the medical advice to the medical experts, unless asked.** You probably don't really know or understand the details of this individual case, and sometimes, alternative "it can't hurt to try" methods really can harm.

- **Don't offload your own trauma.** For those of us who have gone through similar experiences, this is an important tip. Success stories and shared experiences are often a beacon of light and hope. At the same time, be mindful not to offload your own story and trauma without being prompted to do so. Keep in mind that until the family is out of the woods, they are not always capable of listening to the details of others' experiences. They will certainly not be capable of helping you process or heal from your own traumatic hospitalizations.

I made the bad mistake of sharing my own trauma when friends of ours gave birth to a preemie themselves. All giddy and cavalier about our miracle preemie, we lent them a copy of a TV program about preemies we'd been featured on, thinking that they would appreciate it. That program featured three couples: Chaya and me while we were still going through the experience; another couple, whose baby had graduated from the NICU and was doing well; and a couple whose baby, sadly, didn't make it. Cluelessly, I hadn't even considered that part of the program and its impact on a family who had a preemie still sick in the hospital, and I felt terrible when our friends returned it to us, a bit upset at me. I was so intent on telling *my* story that I had not considered their very real and current fears. (Thank G-d, in the end, their preemie did as well as ours did, and they eventually forgave me as well.)

At the same time, both during our preemie's and cardiac kid's hospitalizations, we hung onto success stories. We wanted to hear of the children who beat the odds. We'd look at the pictures of NICU graduates in the fervent hope that our little guy would join them some day. But we were not yet capable of listening to the details, and we certainly were not capable of comforting those who'd gone through traumatic hospitalizations! Mostly, we needed our own somewhat unclear feelings to be validated and sifted through.

The key is to be a sensitive listener and to provide heartfelt encouragement and strength. Don't be a taker; don't absorb energy from someone who needs every ounce of it. Remember, you are there to *lighten* the burden.

Here are some keys to hospital visiting:

- **Coordinate with the family beforehand**, and then double-check when you get to the hospital or home. In medically complex situations, and particularly in the hospital itself, things are often dynamic or unpredictable, so be flexible.
- **Make sure the family knows exactly who is coming** and that they are okay with it. Sometimes, well-meaning friends bring along a toddler or baby, and it causes unnecessary stress; it may be hard to see a healthy child when theirs is fighting for his life. Other times, the family may be worried about germs, or that the rambunctious three-year-old might pull on or trip over a vital

cord or tube. It might also be fine—just clear it with them. No surprises.

- **Visits don't need to be long.** Some people stress out so much about their visit that they find it too hard to stop by ("What will I say? What will I do?"). But the truth is that even ten minutes is valuable; in fact, more than that might not be. Unfortunately, sometimes people create more exhaustion by overstaying their welcome. But when you make it into a short, sweet experience, just enough to express "I care and I'm with you," you will have brought far more than you can possibly believe to the equation in just a short amount of time.

- **A hot meal goes a long way.** Hot soup, in particular, is incredible. We rarely ate a proper, fresh, hot meal when we were in the hospital, and if we did, it was only because a friend brought it to us.

While on the subject of food, I would be remiss if I did not mention all the dinners that the communities in Seattle, Miami, and Boston provided for us over all those long months. Along with that, we were most appreciative of those families that communicated with us in advance about the food. Children can be picky eaters, and letting people know what food they enjoy and what food they will not eat took significant pressure off of us. Shared Excel sheets or websites like TakeThemAMeal.com simplify things quite a bit because the parents can see what food is being offered and when, and they can even create a list of foods their family enjoys. Anything to eliminate frustration or extra work is valuable.

WE KNOW WE COULDN'T HAVE DONE IT without our friends and family. For them, for all the above, and for life itself, we are eternally grateful.

Acknowledgments

A challenging experience like the one we recount in this book can only be endured and overcome with a strong support team. We have been lucky enough to be richly blessed with incredibly giving and dedicated people and organizations that have come through when we've needed them most; not just when we asked, but in multiple ways we didn't even know we needed.

To that end, our most humble attempt at expressing our infinite thanks is extended to:

Our dear parents, R' Leibel and Fraida Estrin, and Rabbi Yaakov and Miriam Karp, who appeared from across the country in a moment's notice to help out during crises, and taught us with their personal example how to handle adversity with faith. No words can fully express our thanks for you, your individual and collective journeys, and the living lessons you've imparted to us with love and wisdom. Having professional writers in the family definitely helps out as well; we hope we did our genes proud!

Our incredible siblings and siblings-in-law for their non-stop encouragement and support. From all the messages and calls, to babysitters showing up right when we were drooping; you guys—and your families—are awesome.

Our precious children, Yehuda, Shayna, Naomi, Levi, and Menachi—for showering Nissi with your boundless love and patience, and being amazing, fun, and resilient troopers on the unexpected journey that his life has taken all of us on. You make us incredibly proud every day.

Our beloved extended family and friends for always showing your deep care and concern. There are way too many of you to be mentioned individually, but we deeply appreciate each and every one of you and your messages of love.

The following outstanding groups and organizations, among others, have been there when we've needed them most. Your professional staffs, selfless volunteers, and vision have changed our lives and those of so many:

Beis Menachem of NMB; Chabad on Campus International and our Chabad on Campus brothers and sisters; Chai Lifeline; Friendship Circle of Miami and Broward County; Healing Hearts; Yaldei Shluchei HaRebbe; YL Hearts—Yeametz Libecha; the Rebbe's Shluchim, particularly our friends and colleagues in the Pacific Northwest, the Western region, Boston area, and Florida; the Seattle, Miami, and Boston Jewish communities; Nissi's endearing fans on Whatsapp and Facebook; all those generous souls who donated to the original Charidy campaign, as well as the pool heater campaign; all the Chabad Houses, schools, and institutions that brought us out to speak; our Aleph Institute and military colleagues.

To the book reviewers: Rabbi Avrohom Blesofsky, Mandy Hakimi, Dr. Sarah Stroup, Rabbi Sholly Weiser, and Yitzi Shollar. Your thoughtful additions, critiques, and feedback brought the book to a whole new level. And to Chaya Rochel's mother, Miriam Karp: your editing skills made this instrument sing beautifully.

A special thanks to Dr. Anthony Rossi, who is not only an erudite and caring cardiologist, but took the time out of his incredibly busy schedule to create the images of Nissi's heart and the various repairs for this book. Dr. Rossi is the consummate mensch.

Thank you does not even begin to touch the surface of our gratitude toward Dr. Files, Dr. McMullan, Dr. Del Nido, and all the other doctors, unheralded nurses, and medical professionals of all types involved in Nissi's care. Thank you for allowing G-d to work His miracles through your attentive and skilled care. We also want to express our gratitude to the numerous therapists who have worked tirelessly to bring Nissi to this point. Our deepest appreciation to his current team at Nicklaus Children's Midtown led by Vanessa Strauss, whose skill, concern, and urgency, alongside their belief in Nissi, have really been above and beyond. We are extraordinarily thankful to have you working with Nissi, and we're looking forward to celebrating his graduation from your care together with you!

Our deepest thanks to all those who joined our Kickstarter campaign to help bring this book to publication. We're extremely grateful to every one of you—and particularly to those of you who generously gave us dedications and sponsorships, including:

Danny and Tovah Ahdut, Ephrayim and Rochel Baskin, Levi Benjaminson, Doniel and Rucheli Berry, Adam Bortz, Michoel and Dassi Brofman, Shimon and Tova Cox, Rabbi Chaim and Kaila Danzinger, Dr. Shimon Dershowitz and Dr. Susan Hankin, Rabbi Matisyahu and Nechama Devlin, MSgt. Mike and Bluma Ekshtut, R' Leibel and Fraida Estrin, Steve and Colette Estrin, Esther Fettman, Abi and Yonati Friedman, Chris Glenn, Jake Goldrich, Rabbi Yaakov and Miriam Karp, Dr. Craig Keebler and Dr. Carol Teitz, Ray and Ruth Kellerman, Andy and Adi Kohn, Binyamin and Mushky Kulek, Rabbi Sholom Ber and Mrs. Chanie Levitin, Mendy and Shternie Lipszyc, Shmuli Lipszyc, Rabbi Shlomo Litvin, Adam and Jennie Minkus, Tony and Robin Mitchell, Drs. Josh and Marianna Newson, Mendel Notik, Daniel Perez, Leyzer and Tikvah Pickett, Rabbi Eli Pink, Yonatan and Natacha Prezman, Ezzy Rappaport, Chezky Rodal, Sarah Yaffa Ross, Avremi Rothman, Michelle Saka, Yonasan and Nechama Sanford, David Smith, Rhonda Snyder, Dr. Rennie Stein, Dr. Sarah Stroup, Gary and Lilly Stute, Dianne Summers, David Weingarten, Rabbi Mendy and Tzippy Weiss, CSM Sam Yudin, Rabbi Avremi Zippel, along with all the rest of our friends who joined forces to bring this book to fruition.

We are very gratified by the assistance we've received from Rav Yaacov Haber and Rabbi Doron Kornbluth of Mosaica Press. Our thanks to Sherie Gross, managing editor; Zahava Berkowitz, copyeditor; Daliya Shapiro, proofreader; Rayzel Broyde, art director, and her highly skilled graphic team; and Henna Eisenman for their hard work to bring this project to completion.

Three artists gave freely of their time and skill: photographers Levik Hertzl and Esti Smith, whose work is found in this volume, and videographer and documentarian Bentzi Avtzon of Yuvla Media, who presented our story with his impressive cinematic storytelling for the online world. We are truly grateful.

Mention must be made to a most special group: friends and family who have been through or are currently going through intense medical journeys of their own, some of whose travails eclipse ours, and others who are no longer with us but remain an eternal inspiration. You are our fellow warriors, and true heroes. This book is dedicated to all of you—particularly to Rafi and Mikey, of blessed memory, and יבדל״א, to Nissi, Mussia, and all the other brave children and parents we've been blessed to meet along the way. You embody true courage on a daily basis. Our deepest, most fervent wish is that the One Above heals all speedily and completely, with the coming of Mashiach.

And finally, to our Rebbe, whose truly boundless G-dly wisdom and sensitivity enrich us on a constant basis. May we merit to bring the Rebbe much *nachas*.

תודה ושבח לא-ל בורא עולם

ברוך א-ל ההודאות

Diagrams of Nissi's Heart Anatomy

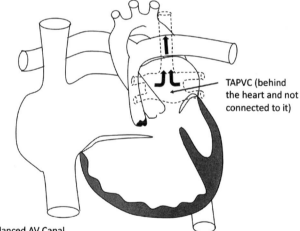

TAPVC (behind the heart and not connected to it)

1. Right Dominant Unbalanced AV Canal
2. Pulmonary Atresia
3. Total Anomalous Pulmonary Venous Connection (TAPVC)

Operation 1

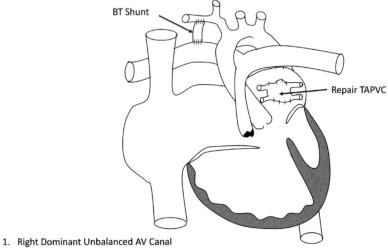

1. Right Dominant Unbalanced AV Canal
2. Pulmonary Atresia
3. Total Anomalous Pulmonary Venous Connection (TAPVC)

Operation 2

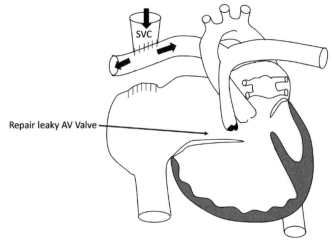

1. Bidirectional Glenn Operation (SVC to Pulmonary Artery Shunt)

Operation 3

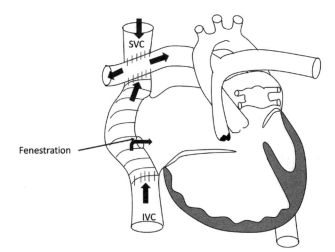

1. Extra Cardiac Fenestrated Fontan

Glossary of Jewish Terms

The following glossary provides a partial explanation of some of the Hebrew, Yiddish (Y.), and Aramaic (A.) words and phrases used in this book. The spellings and explanations reflect the way the specific word is used herein. Often, there are alternate spellings and meanings for the words.

Adar: a Hebrew calendar month, usually corresponding to late winter/ early spring.

aliyah: lit., elevation; the division of the weekly Torah portion into seven sections. When the Torah is read on Saturdays, seven men are called up to the Torah, one for each section.

Amidah: lit., standing; the central daily prayer, consisting of nineteen blessings, mostly of our daily needs.

Baal Shem Tov: lit., Master of the Good Name; name given to Rabbi Israel of Medzhibozh, founder of the Chassidic movement (1698–1760).

bar kayama: (A.) lit., an existing son; a Jewish legal term referring to when a baby is considered fully viable, at thirty days old.

bar mitzvah: (A.) lit., a son of the commandments; a Jewish legal term referring to the age when a male is considered responsible for religious obligations, at thirteen years old.

beit cholim: lit., the house of the sick; hospital.

beit/batei refuah: lit., the house, or houses of the sick.

b'neichem: lit., your son (as in Deuteronomy 11:19).

birkas habanim: lit., the blessing of the children; traditional blessing given to children by the father, in some communities every Friday night, and in others on the eve of Yom Kippur. The text used is from Genesis 40:20 and Numbers 6:22.

bris/bris milah: male circumcision in recognition of the Covenant of Abraham, usually done at eight days old.

Chabad on Campus: a Jewish outreach organization for Jewish students on college campuses.

Chabad representatives: Chabad is a Jewish movement created in the late 1700s. Over the past seventy years, it has been the foremost organization fighting assimilation around the world.

Chai Lifeline: an organization founded in 1987 to help families with children battling deadly diseases.

challah: a braided bread, traditionally eaten at the Sabbath meal.

Chanukah: the winter holiday celebrating the victory of a small group of Jewish warriors over the Seleucid-Greek armies to regain control of Jerusalem and the Temple.

Chassidic: belonging to one of the Hassidic groups stemming from the philosophy of Rabbi Israel Baal Shem Tov.

chevrah kaddisha: (A.) lit., the holy society; Jewish burial society.

Chitat: an acronym for Chumash (the Five Books of Moses); *Tehillim* (Psalms); and *Tanya* (the classic work of Chabad philosophy). All three are divided into daily study.

Chovos Halevavos: *Duties of the Heart*, a classic text written by Rabbi Bachya ibn Paquda (1050–1120).

Chumash: the Five Books of Moses.

dayeinu: lit., it would be enough; a poem sung during the Passover Seder.

Elul: a Hebrew calendar month, occurring at the end of summer/ early fall.

Erev: the day before Sabbath or a holiday.

farbrengen: (Y.) a Chassidic get-together.

Four Species: palm, myrtle, willow, and citron. See Leviticus 23:40.

gemilus chassadim: acts of kindness.

halachah/halachic/halachically: Jewish law, in accordance with.

Hallel: the verses of praise sung on special occasions, consisting of chapters 114–118 in Psalms.

Hashem: lit., the Name; common name for G-d.

Igeres Hakodesh: section four of the classic work *Tanya*.

ipcha mistabranik: (A.) lit., the opposite makes sense; a contrarian.

Kabbalas Shabbos: the prayers welcoming the Sabbath.

Kiddush: lit., sanctification; the prayers recited over wine for the Sabbath and holidays.

kippah: a skullcap.

kosher: the rules governing what food may be eaten according to Jewish law.

kashering: making the kitchen fit to be used for kosher food.

l'chayim: lit., to life; a traditional Jewish toast.

landsleit: (Y.) a countryman.

Lechah Dodi: "Come, my beloved," the opening words of a beautiful song welcoming the Sabbath and recited during the Friday night prayer service, written by Rabbi Shlomo Alkabetz (1500–1576).

levavechem: your heart. See Deuteronomy 11:13.

Lubavitcher Rebbe: Rabbi Menachem Mendel Schneerson (1902–1994), leader of the Chabad-Lubavitch movement.

mazel tov: congratulations.

mezuzahs: the scrolls placed upon the doorposts of Jewish homes. See Deuteronomy 6:9.

minchas ani: lit., a pauper's offering to G-d.

Mishneh Torah: Maimonides' (1138-1204) magnum opus, consisting of a complete legal review of all areas of Jewish law.

mitzvah: lit., a commandment; the responsibilities relegated by G-d to the Jewish people.

Mitzvah Tank: an RV used for the purpose of Jewish outreach.

Modim: lit., thanks or acknowledge; a reference to the seventeenth blessing of the Amidah.

mohel: a ritual circumciser.

Mashiach's Meal: the final meal of the Passover holiday, held in Chassidic tradition to celebrate the imminent arrival of the Messiah.

neis: lit., a miracle.

niggun: a Hassidic tune.

Niggunei Hisva'adus: lit., Songs of the Gatherings; a six-part CD collection of the Lubavitcher Rebbe singing during gatherings he led.

olam: lit., world.

parashah: the section of the Torah read in accordance with the weekly cycle.

Seder: the traditional meal held on Passover to commemorate the Jewish people leaving Egypt.

Purim: the holiday celebrated during late winter/early spring, celebrating the salvation of the Jewish people as recounted in the Book of Esther.

Refa'einu: lit., heal us; the blessing in the *Amidah* asking G-d to heal the sick.

rishon: lit., the first; the term for the first *aliyah* in the weekly Torah portion.

Rosh Chodesh: lit., the head of the month; a mini celebratory day held on the thirtieth and the first days of the Jewish calendar month.

Rosh Hashanah: lit., the head of the year; the fall festival celebrating the Jewish New Year.

sandek: (Y.) the honorary responsibility of holding the baby during his circumcision; godfather.

Sefer Hamitzvos: Maimonides' compilation of the 613 Commandments of the Torah.

seudas hoda'ah: a celebratory meal of thanksgiving.

Shaar Habitachon: Gate of Trust; a section of Rabbi Bachya ibn Paquda's *Chovos Halevavos*.

Shabbos: the Jewish Sabbath, celebrated from sundown on Friday evening until nightfall on Saturday night. During this twenty-five-hour period, it is forbidden to do any biblically mandated "work," which includes many extensions. Modern application precludes the active usage of electricity, such as phones or cars, unless in life-threatening circumstances.

shabbaton: a group Sabbath experience.

shalom: lit., peace.

shalom zachar: a celebration held Friday night after the birth of a baby boy.

Shavuos: the summer holiday celebrating the receiving of the Torah at Mount Sinai.

shayna punim: (Y.) a pretty face.

Shehecheyanu: lit., Who has given us life; the blessing said on special occasions.

Shema: lit., Hear (O Israel); the opening words of the fundamental Jewish prayer that proclaims the unity of G-d, recited in daily prayers and at bedtime. See Deuteronomy 6:4–6:9.

Shevat: a Hebrew calendar month that occurs during the winter time.

shlichus: a mission; term used to describe Chabad emissary outreach work.

shofar: a ram's horn, traditionally blown on Rosh Hashanah.

Simchas Torah: the holiday in the fall celebrating completing and renewing the yearly cycle of reading the Torah.

Sukkah: a booth with a vegetative roof made for the holiday of Sukkos.

Sukkos: the fall holiday reminding the Jewish people of their sojourn in the desert.

tallis: a prayer shawl.

Talmud: an extensive compilation of Jewish law and tradition, compiled after the destruction of the Second Temple.

Tanya: a classic work of Jewish mysticism, written by Rabbi Shneur Zalman Boruchovitch of Liady (1745–1812).

tefillin: phylacteries; the boxes placed upon the head and arm.

Tehillim: the Book of Psalms.

Tinok ben [Chaya Rochel]: lit., Baby the son of [Chaya Rochel]; an anonymous term used prior to a baby receiving a name.

Tishrei: a Hebrew calendar month that occurs in the fall and is full of Jewish holidays.

Torah: the entire corpus of Jewish religious works; a scroll containing the Five Books of Moses.

tov: lit., good.

Tu B'Shevat: the fifteenth day of the month of Shevat; a Jewish arbor day.

Tzemach Tzedek: a book authored by, and nickname given to, Rabbi Menachem Mendel of Lubavitch (1789–1866), the third Rebbe of the Chabad Lubavitch movement (not to be confused with his great-grandson, the seventh Lubavitcher Rebbe, who had the same name).

tzitzis: the fringes worn by Jewish males on the corner of four cornered garments in fulfillment of the Biblical verses in Numbers 15:37–15:40.

upsherenish: (Y.) a boy's first haircut, traditionally given at age three.

yeshiva: a rabbinical school.

Yom Kippur: the Day of Atonement, which falls on the tenth day of Tishrei.

Zohar: the foundational text of Jewish mysticism.

Glossary of Medical Terms

appendectomy: the surgical removal of the appendix.

appendix: a small pouch-like sac of tissue that is located in the first part of the colon (cecum) in the lower-right abdomen. Lymphatic tissue in the appendix aids in immune function.

arrhythmia: a problem with the rate or rhythm of the heartbeat. During an arrhythmia, the heart can beat too fast, too slowly, or with an irregular rhythm.

aspirate: the accidental breathing in of food or fluid into the lungs. This can cause serious health issues, such as pneumonia and other lung problems.

bilirubin: a yellow compound that occurs in the normal catabolic pathway that breaks down heme from hemoglobin, myoglobin, peroxidases, and cytochromes in vertebrates. This catabolism is a necessary process in the body's clearance of waste products that arise from the destruction of aged or abnormal red blood cells.

BT (Blalock-Taussig) shunt: creates a pathway for blood to reach the lungs. A connection is made between the first artery that branches off the aorta (called the right subclavian artery) and the right pulmonary artery. Some of the blood traveling through the aorta toward the body will "shunt" through this connection and flow into the pulmonary artery to receive oxygen.

cardiac arrest: the sudden, unexpected loss of heart function, breathing, and consciousness.

carina: a cartilage situated at the point where the trachea (windpipe) divides into the two bronchi.

catheterization (cath): a procedure used to diagnose and treat certain cardiovascular conditions. During cardiac catheterization, a long thin tube called a catheter is inserted in an artery or vein in your groin, neck, or arm and threaded through your blood vessels to your heart.

cerebral palsy (CP): a group of disorders that affects a person's ability to move and maintain balance and posture. CP is the most common motor disability in childhood. Cerebral means having to do with the brain. Palsy means weakness or problems with using the muscles.

charge nurse: a registered nurse who is essentially in charge of a ward in the hospital or other healthcare facility during their shift. These nurses perform many of the tasks that general nurses do but also have some supervisory duties.

CICU: cardiac intensive care unit.

Code Blue: an emergency situation announced in a hospital or institution in which a patient is in cardiopulmonary arrest, requiring a team of providers (sometimes called a code team) to rush to the specific location and begin immediate resuscitative efforts.

collaterals: Collateral circulation is a network of tiny blood vessels that, under normal conditions, are not open. When the coronary arteries narrow to the point that blood flow to the heart muscle is limited (coronary artery disease), collateral vessels may enlarge and become active.

common valve: the single valve in a single ventricle heart, instead of the four valves found in normal hearts.

congenital heart disease: a problem with the structure of the heart that is present at birth. Congenital heart defects are the most common type of birth defect. The defects can involve the walls of the heart, the valves of the heart, and the arteries and veins near the heart.

Coumadin: (warfarin) an anticoagulant (blood thinner).

COVID-19 coronavirus: the 2019 novel coronavirus outbreak, first identified in Wuhan China. The new name of this disease is coronavirus disease 2019, abbreviated as COVID-19, in which *CO* stands for corona, *VI* for virus, and *D* for disease. Formerly, this disease was referred to as "2019 novel coronavirus" or "2019-nCoV."

CPAP: continuous positive airway pressure; a form of positive airway pressure ventilation in which a constant level of pressure above atmospheric pressure is continuously applied to the upper airway.

CPR: cardiopulmonary resuscitation; an emergency procedure that combines chest compressions often with artificial ventilation in an effort to manually preserve intact brain function until further measures are taken to restore spontaneous blood circulation and breathing in a person who is in cardiac arrest.

CF: cystic fibrosis; a hereditary disorder affecting the exocrine glands. It causes the production of abnormally thick mucus, leading to the blockage of the pancreatic ducts, intestines, and bronchi, often resulting in respiratory infection.

desat episodes: the condition of a low blood oxygen concentration, measured by pulse oximetry.

diaphragm: a dome-shaped muscular partition separating the thorax from the abdomen in mammals. It plays a major role in breathing, as its contraction increases the volume of the thorax and so inflates the lungs.

Dilaudid: a medicine containing hydromorphone, an opioid agonist, and is indicated for the management of pain severe enough to require an opioid analgesic and for which alternative treatments are inadequate.

echocardiogram: a test that uses ultrasound to show how your heart muscle and valves are working. The sound waves make moving pictures of your heart so your doctor can get a good look at its size and shape.

ECMO: extracorporeal membrane oxygenation; an extracorporeal technique of providing prolonged cardiac and respiratory support to persons whose heart and lungs are unable to provide an adequate amount of gas exchange or perfusion to sustain life; also known as extracorporeal life support.

EEG: electroencephalography; an electrophysiological monitoring method to record electrical activity of the brain. It is typically noninvasive, with the electrodes placed along the scalp, although invasive electrodes are sometimes used, as in electrocorticography, sometimes called intracranial EEG.

ER: emergency room.

esophageal atresia: a birth defect in which part of a baby's esophagus (the tube that connects the mouth to the stomach) does not develop properly. Esophageal atresia is a birth defect of the swallowing tube (esophagus) that connects the mouth to the stomach.

esophageal fistula: tracheoesophageal fistula is an abnormal connection in one or more places between the esophagus (the tube that leads from the throat to the stomach) and the trachea (the tube that leads from the throat to the windpipe and lungs). Normally, the esophagus and the trachea are two separate tubes that are not connected.

esophagus: the tube that leads from the throat to the stomach.

extubation: the removal of the breathing tube by a doctor.

fellow: a fellowship is the period of medical training, in the United States and Canada, that a physician, dentist, or veterinarian may undertake after completing a specialty training program (residency). During this time (usually more than one year), the physician is known as a fellow.

Feldenkrais Therapy: a type of exercise therapy devised by Israeli Moshé Feldenkrais during the mid-twentieth century. The method is claimed to reorganize connections between the brain and body, thereby improving body movement and psychological state.

fluoroscopy: a study of moving body structures similar to an X-ray "movie." A continuous X-ray beam is passed through the body part being examined. The beam is transmitted to a TV-like monitor so that the body part and its motion can be seen in detail.

Fontan: a palliative surgical procedure used in children with univentricular hearts. It involves diverting the venous blood from the inferior vena cava (IVC) and superior vena cava (SVC) to the pulmonary arteries without passing through the morphologic right ventricle.

G-tube: gastrostomy tube; a tube inserted through the belly that brings nutrition directly to the stomach. It's one of the ways doctors can make sure kids who have trouble eating get the fluid and calories they need. A surgeon puts in a G-tube during a short procedure called a gastrostomy.

gait trainer: a wheeled device that assists a person who is unable to walk independently to learn or relearn to walk safely and efficiently as part of gait training. Gait trainers are intended for children or adults with physical disabilities, to provide the opportunity to improve walking ability.

GJ-tube: gastro-jejunal tube; a thin, long tube which is threaded into the jejunal (J) portion of the small intestine. GJ-tubes are used for individuals with dysmotility, those who aspirate, and those who are losing a great deal of calories due to vomiting, but who are not good candidates for a fundoplication. Rather than feeding into the stomach like G-tubes, GJ-tubes can be used to bypass the stomach and feed directly into the second portion of the small intestine. The gastric port can be used to give medications, vent air, drain fluids, and give feeds if appropriate and safe for the individual.

Glenn procedure: a palliative surgical procedure, the second of the surgeries to correct the single ventricle heart defect, where the surgeon connects the superior vena cava to the right pulmonary artery.

hairline fracture: a small crack or severe bruise within a bone; also known as a stress fracture.

hematocrit: the volume percentage of red blood cells in blood, measured as part of a blood test; also known by several other names.

hematology: the branch of medicine concerned with the study of the cause, prognosis, treatment, and prevention of diseases related to blood.

hepatologist: a specialist in the branch of medicine that incorporates the study of liver, gallbladder, biliary tree, and pancreas as well as management of their disorders.

heterotaxy: a condition characterized by internal organs that are not arranged in the chest and abdomen as would be expected. Organs are expected to be in a particular orientation inside of the body, known as situs solitus.

hiatal hernia: a condition in which the upper part of the stomach bulges through an opening in the diaphragm. The diaphragm is the thin muscle that separates the chest from the abdomen and helps keep acid from coming up into the esophagus.

HIPAA: Health Insurance Portability and Accountability Act. The term most often refers to the HIPAA Privacy Rule, which establishes national standards to protect individuals' medical records and other personal health information, and applies to health plans, health care clearinghouses, and those health care providers who conduct certain health care transactions electronically.

ICU: intensive care unit.

immunocompromised: reduced ability to fight infections and other diseases.

interventional radiology: a medical specialization that involves performing a range of imaging procedures to obtain images of the inside of the body.

intubated: Tracheal intubation, usually simply referred to as intubation, is the placement of a flexible plastic tube into the trachea to maintain an open airway or to serve as a conduit through which to administer certain drugs.

IV: an intravenous line for providing medication via veins.

L&D: labor and delivery ward.

lactate: a chemical naturally produced by the body to fuel the cells during times of stress. Its presence in elevated quantities is commonly associated with sepsis and severe inflammatory response syndrome. In general, a greater increase in lactate means a greater severity of the condition. When associated with lack of oxygen, an increase in lactate can indicate that organs are not functioning properly.

laparoscopic surgery: a surgical technique in which short, narrow tubes (trocars) are inserted into the abdomen through small (less than one centimeter) incisions. Through these trocars, long, narrow instruments are inserted. The surgeon uses these instruments to manipulate, cut, and sew tissue.

liver atresia: biliary atresia is a rare liver disease that occurs in infants. The disorder affects tubes in the liver called bile ducts. If not treated with surgery, it can be fatal. When a child has biliary atresia, the bile ducts in the liver are blocked. Bile becomes backed up in the liver, damaging the liver and other organs.

Lovenox: an anticoagulant medication. It is used to treat and prevent deep vein thrombosis and pulmonary embolism including during pregnancy and following certain types of surgery. It is also used in those with acute coronary syndrome and heart attacks.

lung lobe: the branches of the lung.

malrotated intestines: an abnormality that can happen early in pregnancy when a baby's intestines don't form into a coil in the abdomen. Malrotation means that the intestines (or bowel) are twisting, which can cause obstruction (blockage).

Methadone: a narcotic that can treat moderate to severe pain. It can also be used to wean off narcotic drug addiction.

MRI: magnetic resonance imaging; a medical imaging technique used in radiology to form pictures of the anatomy and the physiological processes of the body. MRI scanners use strong magnetic fields, magnetic field gradients, and radio waves to generate images of the organs in the body.

nasal cannula/prongs: a device used to deliver supplemental oxygen or increased airflow to a patient or person in need of respiratory help. This device consists of a lightweight tube that on one end splits into two prongs that are placed in the nostrils and from which a mixture of air and oxygen flows.

ND tube: naso-duodenum tube; a tube that goes through the stomach and ends in the first portion of the small intestine (duodenum).

NIRS: near-infrared spectroscopy; a brain imaging method that measures light absorbance to calculate oxy-hemoglobin (oxy-HB) and deoxy-hemoglobin (deoxy-HB), which provides an indirect measure of brain activity, particularly in the frontal cortex.

NICU: neonatal intensive care unit.

neonatologist: the medical specialty of taking care of newborn babies, sick babies, and premature babies.

neurological/neurologist: the study of/a specialist in the anatomy, functions, and organic disorders of nerves and the nervous system.

NG tube: naso-gastric tube; a flexible tube of rubber or plastic that is passed through the nose, down through the esophagus, and into the stomach.

Nissen fundoplication: a procedure in which the gastric fundus (upper part) of the stomach is wrapped, or plicated, around the lower end of the esophagus and stitched in place, reinforcing the closing function of the lower esophageal sphincter. The esophageal hiatus is also narrowed down by sutures to prevent or treat concurrent hiatal hernia, in which the fundus slides up through the enlarged esophageal hiatus of the diaphragm.

OB-GYN: obstetrician/gynecologist.

ostomy: an ostomy pouching system is a prosthetic medical device that provides a means for the collection of waste from a surgically diverted biological system and the creation of a stoma.

oxygen saturation (sats): the fraction of oxygen-saturated hemoglobin relative to total hemoglobin in the blood. The human body requires and regulates a very precise and specific balance of oxygen in the blood. Normal arterial blood oxygen saturation levels in humans are 95–100 percent.

palliative care: an interdisciplinary medical caregiving approach aimed at optimizing quality of life and mitigating suffering among people with serious, complex illness.

PDA: patent ductus arteriosus; a persistent opening between the two major blood vessels leading from the heart. The opening, called the ductus arteriosus, is a normal part of a baby's circulatory system before birth that usually closes shortly after birth.

PT, OT: physical and occupational therapies.

PA: physician's assistant.

PICC line: peripherally inserted central catheter; a form of intravenous access that can be used for long periods of time. It is a catheter that enters the body through the skin at a peripheral site, extends to the superior vena cava, and stays in place within the veins for days or weeks.

PICU: pediatric intensive care unit.

placenta: an organ that develops in the uterus during pregnancy. This structure provides oxygen and nutrients to the growing baby and removes waste products from the baby's blood. The placenta attaches to the wall of the uterus, and the baby's umbilical cord arises from it.

POLST: Physician's Order for Life-Sustaining Treatment; a doctor's order not to resuscitate.

preemie: a prematurely born baby.

probiotics: live microorganisms that provide health benefits when consumed, generally by improving or restoring the gut flora.

prostaglandin: powerful, locally-acting vasodilators that inhibit the aggregation of blood platelets. Through their role in vasodilation, prostaglandins are also involved in inflammation. They are synthesized in the walls of blood vessels and serve the physiological function of preventing needless clot formation, as well as regulating the contraction of smooth muscle tissue.

PTSD: post-traumatic stress disorder.

pulmonary artery: carries deoxygenated blood from the right ventricle to the lungs. The blood here passes through capillaries adjacent to alveoli and becomes oxygenated as part of the process of respiration.

pulmonary atresia: a form of heart disease in which the pulmonary valve does not form properly. It is present from birth (congenital heart disease). The pulmonary valve is an opening on the right side of the heart that regulates blood flow from the right ventricle (right side pumping chamber) to the lungs.

pulmonary flow: the blood flow from the heart to the lungs.

pulmonary valve: the valve of the heart that lies between the right ventricle and the pulmonary artery.

pulmonary veins: the veins that transfer oxygenated blood from the lungs to the heart. The largest pulmonary veins are the four main pulmonary veins, two from each lung that drain into the left atrium of the heart.

pulse-oximeter: a tiny device that uses infrared light refraction to measure how well oxygen is binding to your red blood cells.

reflux: a common condition that features a burning pain, known as heartburn, in the lower chest area. It happens when stomach acid flows back up into the food pipe. Gastroesophageal reflux disease (GERD) is diagnosed when acid reflux occurs more than twice a week.

residents: residency or postgraduate training is a specific stage of graduate medical education usually in a hospital or clinic, under the direct or indirect supervision of a senior medical clinician registered in that specialty. Residency training may be followed by fellowship or sub-specialty training.

respiratory therapist: a specialized healthcare practitioner trained in critical care and cardio-pulmonary medicine in order to work therapeutically with people suffering from acute critical conditions, cardiac, and pulmonary disease.

rounds: when various disciplines come together to discuss the patient's condition and coordinate care. The attending physician usually leads or facilitates rounds. A resident, nurse, and a team of allied healthcare professionals are also often in attendance, such as a respiratory therapist, nutritionist, and social worker. Usually the patient's case is presented to the group by either the resident or the nurse. The results of medical procedures, such as X-rays, CT scans, and electrocardiograms may be discussed. Lab work, such as blood and urine tests, will also be reviewed. The plan of care including prioritizing treatment and establishing goals will be evaluated.

RSV: respiratory syncytial virus; a common, and very contagious, virus that infects the respiratory tract of most children before their second birthday. For most babies and young children, the infection causes nothing more than a cold. But for a small percentage, infection with RSV can lead to serious, sometimes life-threatening problems such as pneumonia or bronchiolitis, an inflammation of the small airways of the lungs.

seizures: a sudden, uncontrolled electrical disturbance in the brain.

SIDS: sudden infant death syndrome; the sudden and unexplained death of a baby younger than one year old. A diagnosis of SIDS is made if the baby's death remains unexplained even after a death scene investigation, an autopsy, and a review of the clinical history.

spleen: the largest organ in the lymphatic system. It is an important organ for keeping bodily fluids balanced, but it is possible to live without it. The **spleen** is located under the ribcage and above the stomach in the left upper quadrant of the abdomen.

Subclinical: that which does not present any clinical signs or symptoms.

superior vena cava: the superior of the two venae cavae, the great venous trunks that return deoxygenated blood from the systemic circulation to the right atrium of the heart. It is a large-diameter (24 mm) short-length vein that receives venous return from the upper half of the body, above the diaphragm.

SVT: supraventricular tachycardia; a rapid heartbeat that develops when the normal electrical impulses of the heart are disrupted.

tachypnea: breathing that is abnormally rapid and often shallow.

TAPVC: total anomalous pulmonary venous connection; a rare congenital malformation in which all four pulmonary veins do not connect normally to the left atrium. Instead the four pulmonary veins drain abnormally to the right atrium (right upper chamber) by way of an abnormal (anomalous) connection.

Unbalanced AV canal: complete atrioventricular canal (CAVC); a severe congenital heart disease in which there is a large hole in the tissue (the septum) that separates the left and right sides of the heart. The hole is in the center of the heart, where the upper chambers (the atria) and the lower chambers (the ventricles) meet.

trachea: the windpipe, one part of the airway system. Airways are pipes that carry oxygen-rich air to the lungs. They also carry carbon dioxide, a waste gas, out of the lungs. When one inhales, air travels from the nose, through the larynx, and down the windpipe.

transfusion: the process of transferring blood or blood products into one's circulation intravenously.

valve regurgitation: a backflow of blood caused by failure of the heart's valve to close tightly.

ventilator: a machine that provides mechanical ventilation by moving breathable air into and out of the lungs, delivering breaths to a patient who is physically unable to breathe or is breathing insufficiently.

ventricle: one of two large chambers toward the bottom of the heart that collect and expel blood received from an atrium toward the peripheral beds within the body and lungs.

For Further Reading

Kalmenson, Mendel. *Positiviy Bias*, Ezra Press, 2019.

Rosner, Fred. *Modern Medicine and Jewish Ethics*, Yeshiva University Press, 1986.

The Chassidic Heritage Series. *Full Devotion*, Kehot Publication Society, 2017.

Wineberg, Sholom B. *Healthy in Body, Mind and Spirit*, Sichos in English, 2006.

About the Authors

Rabbi Elie and Chaya Rochel Estrin served as the co-directors of Chabad at University of Washington in Seattle for thirteen years. After moving to North Miami Beach, FL, Rabbi Estrin became the Military Personnel Liaison for the Aleph Institute, combining his Jewish outreach experience with his military position as a Chaplain in the United States Air Force Reserve. Rabbi Estrin also teaches at the Chaya Aydel Seminary in Hallandale Beach, FL, and is a sought-after inspirational speaker. When Chaya Rochel is not serving as Nissi's medical coordinator, chauffeur, and multi-disciplinary therapist alongside being the mom for their other five children, she works in data management.

In honor of our loving parents, grandparents,
and great-grandparents

Gertrude and William Abramson

Zev ben Aaron

Gittel bas Yisrael

Remembering you and loving you always

DEBBIE AND AVI VAKNIN

CHANI, ELDAR, AND LIAM AHARONI

LEETAL AND DAVID GRUBERGER

SHACHAR VAKNIN

In honor of

Nissi

and in honor of

All our nieces and nephews,
grand-nieces, and grand-nephews

STEVE AND COLETTE ESTRIN

Dedicated to our parents with love and blessings
for long life and happy, healthy years until 120

Kayla bas Yehuda
Avinoam ben Avraham
Batsheva bas Moshe
Tzurishaddai ben Avraham

ROB AND ANNA SANFORD

YONASAN AND SARA SANFORD

Dedicated by

DR. CRAIG KEEBLER

Dear Rabbi Elie and Chaya,

Thank you so much for the Torah you taught us in classes, and so much more so through your actions. We look at the strength and integrity with which you live your life, especially as demonstrated by how you never gave up on Nissi even when all the world was saying there was no hope.

You so clearly demonstrated what it means to believe in Hashem with all your heart, all your might, and all your money. It shows us what we can and must live up to.

I'll never forget when I worked with a pediatric cardiologist who didn't know that I knew you and yet said to me, "A rabbi once told me, 'Our job as doctors is to heal and treat, not to predict the future.'"

No matter how dire the situation, because of the courage and perseverance you modeled, I know that every patient in front of me has the chance to live, even a life full of joy.

DRS. JOSH AND MARIANNA NEWSON

Dedicated to

Nissi

the kid with the world's biggest heart

DR. RENNIE STEIN

In memory of our grandparents

Tova bas Carl
and Zev ben Zalmen HaKohen Jacobs

Charna bas Refoel
and Fishel Hirsch ben Yisroel
HaKohen Kussner

And in honor of all of our children,
who are keeping the torch burning bright

DONIEL AND RUCHELI BERRY

Blessings to

the Estrin family

for *hatzlachah*, success,
and strength in all their endeavors

With our warmest wishes,

RUTH AND RAY KELLERMAN AND FAMILY

Dedicated to

Nissi and the Estrin family

RABBI SHOLOM BER AND CHANIE LEVITIN
AND FAMILY

Dedicated to

Anyone reading or receiving
this book who is in need of a berachah

SHIMON AND TOVA COX

With infinite thanks to Hashem
for Your boundless *berachos*.

With love and admiration to

Nissi

and your dear indefatigable parents

and your amazing siblings
Yehuda, Shayna, Naomi, Levi, and Menachi

The greatest team!

All our love,

ZAIDY AND BUBBY KARP

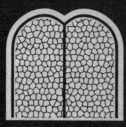

MOSAICA PRESS
BOOK PUBLISHERS

Elegant, Meaningful & Bold

info@MosaicaPress.com
www.MosaicaPress.com

The Mosaica Press team of
acclaimed editors and designers
is attracting some of the most
compelling thinkers and teachers
in the Jewish community today.
Our books are available around
the world.

HARAV YAACOV HABER
RABBI DORON KORNBLUTH